Dive Right In–
The Sharks Won't Bite

**The Entrepreneurial Woman's
Guide to Success**

Jane Wesman

Dearborn
Financial Publishing, Inc.

While a great deal of care has been taken to provide accurate and current information, the ideas, suggestions, general principles and conclusions presented in this text are subject to local, state and federal laws and regulations, court cases and any revisions of same. The reader is thus urged to consult legal counsel regarding any points of law— this publication should not be used as a substitute for competent legal advice.

Executive Editor: Bobbye Middendorf
Managing Editor: Jack Kiburz
Associate Project Editor: Stephanie Schmidt
Interior Design: Lucy Jenkins
Cover Design: Design Alliance, Inc.
Cover Background Photo: © 1995 PhotoDisc, Inc.
Author Photos: Jerry Bauer

Published by Dearborn Financial Publishing, Inc.

Printed in the United States of America

95 96 97 10 9 8 7 6 5 4 3 2 1

Library of Congress Cataloging-in-Publication Data

Wesman, Jane.
    Dive right in—the sharks won't bite : the entrepreneurial woman's guide to success / by Jane Wesman.
        p.   cm.
    Includes index.
    ISBN 0-7931-1101-3 (Cloth)
    1. Women in business—United States. 2. Entrepreneurship—United States. 3. Success in business—United States. I. Title.
HD6054.3.W46 1995   95-10672
658.4'21'082—dc20   CIP

Dedication

For my parents, who taught me to believe that nothing is beyond my grasp.

And for Don, who is always there when I need him.

Acknowledgments

I would like to thank everyone who spent time talking with me, sharing ideas, anecdotes and expertise. Without you, this book would not exist. In particular, I want to thank Arlynn Greenbaum for reading the manuscript in all its permutations; Lori Ames Stuart for her insight and loyalty; Julie Lewit-Nirenberg for her advice and friendship; Patrice Tanaka for her generosity, particularly for sharing her thoughts on hiring and motivating employees; and Bobbye Middendorf for guiding this project through to completion.

Note: Although many of the women I interviewed for *Dive Right In—The Sharks Won't Bite* encouraged me to use their real names, others preferred to remain anonymous. In those instances, I used pseudonyms and changed the specifics of their businesses to maintain their privacy.

—Jane Wesman

Contents

Preface

*D*ive Right In—*The Sharks Won't Bite* is a book for women—for those of you who are considering business ownership or becoming freelance consultants and for those of you who have been in business for several years. The book is designed to help you turn your ideas and aspirations into business success.

I've based the material in *Dive Right In* on my 15 years of experience as an entrepreneur and owner of Jane Wesman Public Relations as well as on the experiences of my friends, colleagues and competitors throughout the country. I've also gathered information from the women I've met working with such organizations as the American Woman's Economic Development Corporation and the Fashion Institute of Technology's Small Business Center. Through these sources, dozens of women in all stages of business development, from start-up to smooth sailing, have told me about their reasons for launching their companies, their struggles and fears, their dreams and suc-

cesses, as well as their day-to-day operations. I've also interviewed experts—accountants, lawyers, psychologists—to round
out the advice you'll find within these pages.

If you've just begun to think about starting a business, turn to
Chapter 1 to learn about the three characteristics of entrepreneurial women—courage, energy and determination—and how
to tap these qualities within yourself. Chapter 2 will help you
evaluate your motives, goals, skills and experience while getting
you to focus on your potential market and initial financing possibilities. Chapter 3 presents creative ways to find the money
you'll need to launch your venture.

Those of you who are already in business may want to skim
the first few chapters of the book and move on to Chapter 4,
which examines the pros and cons of working from home ver-
sus renting an office and presents specific advice on leasing
space. Chapter 5 is filled with practical tips for getting the most
from your accountant or lawyer, and Chapter 6 will help you
hire the right employees. Chapter 7 will show you how to motivate employees for peak performance.

The rest of the book is aimed at women entrepreneurs with
all levels of experience. There are hints for effective networking,
ideas for creating high-performance promotional materials, and
advice on advertising and publicity. You'll also find chapters on
selling and on collecting money—the bane of women business
owners everywhere—plus information on getting organized and
overcoming workaholism. The final chapter is my favorite. It
contains 18 surefire strategies for winning in today's competitive
business world.

Dive Right In is not meant to be read in one sitting. Take it
with you on your journey to entrepreneurial success. Refer to it
as your company grows, as you need to overcome obstacles or
implement new strategies. The next decade will provide many
exciting opportunities for small businesses, and this is the perfect time for women entrepreneurs to dive right in and take
advantage of them all. I wish you the best of luck on your entrepreneurial journey. It is bound to be one of the most thrilling
adventures of your life.

Are You Ready To Dive Right In?

You'll Need Courage, Energy and Determination To Succeed

Entrepreneurship can change your life forever. It can free you from a dull and unfulfilling job. It can give you the flexibility to work at home or in an office. It allows you to set your own hours, hire your own staff and pursue the career path of your dreams. Entrepreneurship can also mean making more money and having fun while you're doing it. But entrepreneurship does not come easily, especially in the beginning. There are numerous hurdles to overcome and countless sacrifices to make. How do you know if you're ready to take the plunge and open your own business? Start with this quiz:

1. Do you hate going to work in the morning?

2. Have you hit the glass ceiling at your company and realized that even a move to another firm will only be a lateral one?

3. Are you a competent and successful employee, yet you feel dissatisfied or unfulfilled in your job?

4. Do you hate the corporate structure and atmosphere?

5. Have you discovered a market niche for a product or service that you know you can fill?

6. Have you worked for a company long enough to have developed a reasonable number of business contacts, some of whom might work directly with you if you start your own enterprise?

7. Do you want to be your own boss?

8. Have you been fired and found that the job market for a woman with your experience looks dismal?

9. Does someone have great faith in you and want to back you in a new venture?

10. Do you need a more flexible schedule to combine work and family responsibilities?

11. Do you want to be rich, or at least make more money than you're making now?

12. Do you dream of running your own company and insist that nothing can stop you until you succeed?

If, like millions of other women, you answered yes to at least three of the preceding questions, then you've probably been bitten by the entrepreneurial bug. Odds are you're going to strike out on your own sometime soon. This book will help you succeed.

What Does It Take To Launch Your Own Business?

Every woman entrepreneur has her own reasons for starting a business. Many have told me that they knew intuitively that it was the right thing to do. The circumstances of their lives led them to it. Some just fell into it. Others said that they wanted more time and flexibility. Some, like myself, were fed up with the corporate world. Other women—and this is happening more and more—were unceremoniously laid off and couldn't find suitable employment. Still others simply had a dream and followed it.

Their reasons may have been different, but what all of these women had in common was courage, energy and determination to succeed. Of course, having a great business plan or a terrific new product or service is important. But without courage, energy and determination, none of these other things guarantees success.

Courage Is Your Number One Ally

Courage comes from deep within you. It is the ability to withstand difficulty, fear or danger. When you start a business, courage is your number one ally, and as a woman, you'll need more of it than a man to become a successful entrepreneur.

Men have been running their own enterprises since time immemorial. Women have not. We have very few role models compared to men. It's a lot easier for a man to look around him and say, "Joe over there owns a hardware store. Steve makes a mint as a management consultant. And Pat runs his own insurance agency. They're all doing well. Why can't I?" It seems common and acceptable for men to be entrepreneurs. It's just starting to look that way for women. We still have many barriers to overcome, particularly our own fears and the fears of those closest to us.

Fight Fear

Deciding to start your own business is a frightening experience. You'll spend your days seeking advice, making plans, asking yourself if you should really do it. You'll spend your nights tossing and turning. This is an important time to surround yourself with supportive people.

You may notice, however, that some of those closest to you—your parents, your husband, your boyfriend or others—begin to give you negative feedback when you tell them you want to strike out on your own. They may be jealous or they may be afraid that they will lose you if you become too successful. Whether their message is subtle or obvious, it will have a tendency to undermine your ambitions. When you start a business, you will need not only the courage to overcome your own fears, but also the courage to listen to what friends and family say and decide for yourself whether they're right or wrong. If they're wrong, you will need courage to forge ahead.

Trust Your Instincts

When Sue Williams launched her Chicago-based consulting firm, she hired a prominent graphic designer to create her company logo. The logo was handsome, corporate-looking and reeked of success. When she showed the sample to her businessman father, he told her not to use it because it was too bold, too masculine and would give people the wrong impression. Now, this is a man who had always insisted that she could be anything she wanted. Yet once she decided to start a business, he was afraid she would project too strong an image.

Sue valued her father's opinions, so she asked another designer to soften the logo, to "feminize" it. After several months and several watered-down versions, she finally realized that the original logo was perfect. She has used it for more than ten years now to create a strong business identity for her company, which today grosses nearly half a million dollars annually. It may seem like a small thing, but Sue told me that it really took courage to decide that her father's advice was wrong.

Trusting your instincts, as Sue Williams did, is one way to tap your inner reserves of courage. Believing in yourself is another. If you feel that you're being undermined by someone who is important in your life, then talk it out. Don't let another person's fears erode your own sense of courage.

Believe in Yourself

About five years ago, when Marilyn Green quit her job at an advertising agency to launch her own business, she decided to announce her plans at her annual Thanksgiving dinner. But just as her relatives began to arrive, her husband whispered, "Don't tell anyone about your new business yet." When Marilyn asked why, he replied, "Just in case you fail. That way you won't be embarrassed." Marilyn was flabbergasted, but agreed to follow her husband's advice.

As the dinner progressed and relatives asked how things were going at her job, Marilyn brushed off their questions. It became obvious that something was amiss. She finally confessed to a cousin that she had decided to fulfill her dreams and start her own business. Her cousin told the others and everyone insisted on hearing more.

Afterward, Marilyn discussed the incident with her husband, explaining how his negative attitude undermined her. He said he was trying to protect her from failure. He felt that if she was unhappy at work, she should find a different job, not start a business.

He didn't have the courage, or the faith in her, that she had. Although this was painful for Marilyn to discover, she still believed in herself enough to persevere. She knew that she was the only person who could make her business succeed, and her courage would have to be enough for both of them. In the end, her husband realized his mistake and became one of her company's biggest supporters. Today, Marilyn's advertising agency is in full bloom, with nearly $10 million dollars in billings.

These two stories are just the tip of the iceberg when it comes to courage. As you read *Dive Right In*, you'll see that courage is a major theme whether you're trying to obtain financing, hire or fire employees, negotiate contracts or just survive in a tough marketplace. Courage is essential to success.

Energy Is Key

Another key quality is energy. Running a business takes huge amounts of time and energy and lots of hard work. Being well organized and having plenty of self-discipline can help to maximize your energy levels, but that's not enough.

Create Energy Through Exercise and Diet

I asked Julie Lewit-Nirenberg, publisher of *Mademoiselle* magazine and one of the busiest women I know, where she gets her huge reserves of energy. Exercise, a low-fat diet and regular amounts of sleep allow her to spend about 30 percent of her business life traveling to cities throughout the United States and Europe to oversee her large sales force. The rest of her business time is spent in high-pressure meetings and consultations.

Julie wakes up at six every morning and jogs or goes to the gym. If she misses her morning exercise, she works out at night. I once spent a weekend at her country home, and I couldn't believe her pace. By the time I awoke at eight, she had already completed a ten-mile bicycle ride and was ready to take me to an aerobics class. Later that day, we played two hours of tennis. Then she took a walk before dinner.

Julie's exercise regimen certainly pays off. She's rarely sick, and she's always energetic and alert. Not every women entrepreneur needs to follow such a strict program, but I advise anyone who wants to feel good to join a health club or take up a sport. (Brisk walking for half an hour a day is a sport as far as I'm concerned.) Exercise clears your head and helps you think more creatively about your business. Health clubs, tennis clubs and golf clubs are also great places to network.

A low-fat diet is the second element in the energy equation. There are many diet or eating programs you can follow. Choose one that works for you—one that you'll stick to. See a nutrition-ist, if necessary, and take vitamins. If you don't eat properly you'll have trouble concentrating and getting your job done.

See Appendix B for a list of health spas, books and videos to help you increase your energy level.

Determination Keeps Courage Alive

Courage and determination go hand in hand. If courage is the ability to withstand difficulty, fear or danger, then determina-tion is what keeps courage going through time. It is the ability to decide what you want to do and then stick to it. I've noticed when working with budding business owners that the ones who succeed are the ones who decide early on what type of busi-ness they want to launch and what niche they want to fill.

Pursue One Business Opportunity Full Force

I met a charming young woman at a seminar I was running who wanted to start a travel agency. At the same time she wanted to be an artist's representative or an image consultant. She spent so much time daydreaming and then trying to do a little of each that she never got any of these businesses off the ground. If she had chosen just one of these fields to start, she would eventu-ally have had time and money to explore other options.

On the other hand, Teri Jacobson, who owns a medical video company, has lots of determination. She began her career film-ing sports events in Salt Lake City, where she grew up. An avid skier and adventure lover, Teri was known as the only woman around who could ski and carry a heavy video camera. This was the ideal job for her.

All was going well until she had a freak accident while film-ing a ski race. One of the racers lost control and hit her, dislo-cating her shoulder and tearing the nerves that fed the muscles of her hand, arm, back and neck. Although the injury healed, Teri suffered severe pain and could work only sporadically after that. She spent years searching for help, undergoing numerous operations to ease the pain and keep her shoulder from dislocating over and over again.

But nothing seemed to help. Some doctors went so far as to say that nothing was wrong and that her pain was psychological. Even her friends began to doubt her. But Teri was determined to put an end to her pain and get her career back on track. After nearly a decade, she found a team of surgeons in the Denver area who were able to help her.

Be Ready To Make Sacrifices

During her recovery, Teri realized that the time had come to rethink her career. Filming ski races and other sports events was too dangerous for her. She needed to find a new way to use her video skills. By coincidence, the physicians who had operated on her were looking for someone to film their innovative surgical procedures to create teaching videos for other doctors. This meant developing a special camera system that could get wet, be sterilized and take pictures of the surgical instruments at work without distortion. After all her suffering, Teri decided this was the job for her.

Teri had to give up her life in Salt Lake City and move to Denver to work on the project. "It was very lonely at first," she recalls, "but I was determined to make it work. I left behind everything I knew—friends, family, the comforts of a hometown. But it's opened up a whole new world to me." Working with the surgical team, Teri has produced a series of videos that have been shown in the United States, Europe and Japan. Her company, now located in Colorado, is doing well, and she's in the midst of developing many new projects. Teri's determination is an inspiration to all women entrepreneurs.

Entrepreneurship: The Adventure of a Lifetime

You will need courage, energy and determination to succeed as an entrepreneur. Be honest with yourself. Do you have the courage to overcome obstacles? The energy to persevere during both good and bad times? The determination to stick it out over the long run? If so, then you're in for the adventure of your life. As an entrepreneur you'll learn to tap inner resources you never knew you had. You'll gain a sense of fulfillment and satisfaction. And best of all, you'll never have to work for anyone else again.

This book will help you to join the ranks of American women who have taken their business destinies into their own hands. It will show you how to deal with day-to-day business issues and how to overcome the stumbling blocks that are unique to women entrepreneurs.

You are not alone on your journey to entrepreneurial success. Today, there are 6 million women business owners in the United States. By the end of this decade, there will be many more. Welcome to their ranks.

CHAPTER 2

Getting Started

Evaluate Your Motives, Goals, Skills and Experience

How do you actually start a business? First, you decide what you want to do. To help you focus, I have prepared a quiz to evaluate your motives, goals, skills and experience. It will get you thinking about your target market and how you're going to finance your new venture. If you're in the early stages of launching a business, this exercise will be very useful.

What Do You Want To Do?

Answer the following questions in writing as thoughtfully as you can. If necessary, take several days to mull them over. There are no right or wrong answers here. The object is to help you find direction in your working life, and to choose the type of business that's right for you.

1. What do I want from my working life? More money? Greater job satisfaction? More free time for family or other interests? Do I want it now or later? Is starting a business the answer?

2. When I think about my life 15 or 20 years from now, what do I imagine? Do I want to be famous? Rich? Running a company? Retired? Living in the country surrounded by my family and pets? Working six months a year, on vacation the rest of the time? How will I reach these goals?

3. What do I like to do? (Think of all the things you do that make you happy. Imagine incorporating them into a job. Some of your favorite activities might include selling, working with numbers, cooking, exercising, writing, teaching, helping others or reading, to name a few.)

4. What are my skills? (Some of your skills will be things you like to do. Others may be things that you don't like to do but that are useful in launching a business. Once you start your business, you can hire people to do some of the things you don't like.)

5. Am I good at working alone, or do I need to be around other people to feel motivated? How does this affect my choice of business?

6. Do I like being in charge, and do I know how to motivate others? Am I good at delegating work and getting people to stick to deadlines? (Successful entrepreneurs know how to motivate others.)

7. Can I afford to give up a weekly paycheck to go out on my own?

8. How will I finance a new business? (You will need less capital to launch a service business than a retail or manufacturing business. See Chapter 3 for specific ideas on start-up financing.)

9. Who are my business contacts? (This is essential in starting a business. Key contacts are people who will buy
your product or service, people who will lend you money
to start your business and experienced people who can
give you solid advice.)

10. How do I know whether there is a market for my product or service? (Asking three or four friends if they would
buy your product or service isn't enough. Do you have
any information on your potential market, either from
personal experience or from experts? Even without specific information, some women have been able to succeed on intuition about the market. Are you convinced
that a market exists for you?)

11. Do I have the courage, energy and determination to
start a business?

Consider Your Options

Spend some time thinking about the answers to the preceding questions. Analyze your motives and your goals. If your
major goal is to make more money, are you certain that running
your own company is the best solution? Perhaps going back to
school or getting a graduate degree in business or law will lead
to greater financial rewards. If your goal is to find more time for
your family, perhaps a new job with flexible hours is the answer.

What about the things you like to do? Make a list, and ask
yourself whether you need to run your own company in order
to do them. For example, if you want to design clothing or
accessories, do you insist on manufacturing them yourself, or
would you be happy designing them for someone else? If you
like to teach aerobics, can you work at a health club, or would
you rather be independent and work with private clients?

What about your working style? If you prefer to be surrounded
by others, can you afford to hire employees right from the start,
or should you try to form a partnership with another entrepre-

neur? If you're not good at delegating, should you give up the idea of business ownership, or should you try to work on your own as an independent contractor?

Whatever you want to do, ask yourself whether you have the skills associated with that industry. Are you good on the phone? Do you know how to sell? What about recordkeeping? Which skills do you have? Which should you acquire? What duties can be handled by someone else? Do you have enough experience in your field, or a related one, to launch your enterprise?

The Value of Experience

Imagine, for example, that you want to start a bakery. Think of the difficulties you will have if your only experience has been baking for your family and friends. You will have to figure out what type of equipment to buy, what quantities of ingredients to order, how many cakes and pastries to bake each day. On top of this, you will face all the other problems of starting a business—financing, renting space, acquiring the proper licenses or permits, buying insurance, hiring an accountant or lawyer, dealing with employees and much more.

But if you had already managed a bakery or had worked for a caterer, restaurant or other related business, you would be way ahead of the game. You would also know whether you really liked baking as a business. Perhaps it's fun on a small scale. As a business, it might be overwhelming.

Kerrie Buitrago, who with her former husband owned Pierrot, a gourmet pastry shop in Brooklyn Heights, is emphatic about the need for relevant experience, saying, "Before opening the shop, I was trained at one of the best cooking schools in Europe, and then I apprenticed at one of the most famous pastry shops in Belgium. Yet as soon as we opened our own place in Brooklyn, I realized that I lacked some essential experience. I would have been better off if I had spent time working in an American pastry shop before launching Pierrot. The way we do business here is completely different from the way it is done in

Europe. I wasn't prepared for that. Although I did catch on, some American training would have saved me a lot of headaches."

Experience Means More Than Basic Skills

Experience means more than just gaining basic business skills or learning about a specific profession. It is also a way to expand your network of contacts. Contacts are the people who will buy from you, encourage you, supply you with services and advice, introduce you to new ideas and opportunities.

Clara Aich, a top New York photographer, was in her early twenties when she moved to the United States to launch her career. Although she was extremely talented and wanted to work on her own, she had little hands-on experience and no contacts, so she accepted a job as a photographer's assistant.

The job was not always pleasant. "I did whatever my employer asked of me," she explains. "When he went on location, I packed his bags and carried his equipment. He acted as if I were invisible." Despite the drawbacks of the job, Clara persevered. She knew the experience was invaluable.

For the next few years, Clara continued building her skills and her network of contacts. By the time she was ready to work independently, she had established a large network of prospective clients, suppliers, mentors and friends. She began her independent career slowly, renting a small studio, buying equipment and hiring employees as she could afford to. As time passed, her reputation grew and she started landing big, lucrative jobs working for some of the world's most famous fashion and cosmetic companies. Today, she and her staff work out of a large studio in a beautiful old carriage house that she owns. Demand for her services is so great that she often has to turn down work.

In looking back on her career, Clara says, "I would have loved to work on my own as soon as I moved to New York, but how could I have kept things going? Where would I have found clients? How would I have set fees or dealt with problems? All of that takes experience. I gained that working for others. Young people today aren't patient enough," she adds. "They want everything given to them right away. They underestimate the value of time and experience."

You Can Never Have Too Much Experience

Clara is not the only one who believes in the value of hands-on experience. In fact, Mildred Freer, a colleague of mine who owns a successful public relations agency in Phoenix, believes you can never have too much of it. Although she had spent 15 years as a public relations executive in a Fortune 500 company when she launched her business, she had no experience working in an agency. "I understood public relations, but I didn't know much about the daily operations of an agency—selling, billing procedures and pricing, for example," she explains. "So I decided to accept a part-time job in a big public relations agency at the same time that I was launching my own business."

Mildred worked there for six months, with the understanding that she would soon be on her own. "It was the best thing I could have done. Not only did I learn a tremendous amount about how to prepare proposals and reports, about contracts and billing procedures, but I also developed solid business relationships with other account executives at the agency. For months after I left, they continued to recommend their overflow business to me." Those recommendations accounted for nearly a third of Mildred's business during her first two years as an entrepreneur.

Ways To Augment Experience

If you don't have experience in your chosen field, there are several options. Try working part-time or as a volunteer or intern, although you must be careful not to undervalue your services by working too long without pay. You can supplement this hands-on experience by attending business seminars or taking courses geared to your industry or to the general problems of small businesses. Appendix D of this book lists graduate schools of business that offer concentrations in entrepreneurship. There is also a list of organizations that offer courses for women entrepreneurs and mentoring programs in which an experienced businessperson will give you advice and guidance. Check them out. Despite fantasies to the contrary, very few people succeed on their own without work experience, training or counseling.

Identify Your Market

At this stage in your plans, it's also time to think about your market. Who will buy your products or services? If you already have experience in your field, then you probably know the answer. Mildred Freer knew who her prospective clients were. They included the Fortune 500 company where she previously worked as well as her colleagues at other corporations who hired public relations consultants. Clara Aich also knew her market before she started working independently. She had met many prospective clients while she assisted other photographers.

What happens if you don't know who your customers are? If you have enough money, you can hire a consultant to prepare a detailed market study. If not, you can create your own informal market survey by pinpointing your prospective clients and discovering what they think of your new product or service.

Let's imagine that you want to design high-fashion hats to be sold in upscale boutiques and department stores. Your experience has been as an editorial assistant at a women's fashion magazine. You have a great eye for design, and you know intuitively that women will like your hats, but will they buy them?

Begin by producing a few hats and try selling them to friends and acquaintances. Present your samples at small gatherings, and ask your guests for feedback. Be prepared with a list of questions. What do they like or not like about your hats? Ask about style, color, comfort, size, materials. Find out how much they're willing to spend on hats and what induces them to buy.

You will also need to visit the stores that you want to carry your merchandise. Do they sell hats like yours? What is the price range? Do they have a large turnover? (You'll need to go back several times to learn the answer to this.) Can you produce hats that will fit their merchandising needs? Think about how you would persuade buyers to take a chance on your designs.

You may decide that there is a market for your hats in boutiques and department stores, or you may decide that the market is flooded. If you decide the latter, don't give up. Try to rethink your start-up strategy. For more information on market research, read Laurie B. Zuckerman's *On Your Own: A Woman's Guide To Building a Business* (Upstart, 1990). This is an excellent book filled with solid advice, worksheets and checklists.

Financing Can Affect Your Business Choice

Another factor to consider is financing. Many women postpone their dreams because they don't have enough money to launch the exact business they want. If capital is a stumbling block, review your goals and see if there is another way to structure your business. Let me give you an example.

I know a woman who desperately wants to manufacture jewelry. She has been obsessed with the idea for three years now, but she will never get her business off the ground. The reason? She insists on producing extremely expensive gold jewelry. She has created all of her designs, but she can't find the capital— $250,000—that she needs to produce her samples. And none of the buyers at department and jewelry stores will order from her until she can show them finished product.

People have suggested that she produce her samples in silver or goldplate, which is less costly, or that she design a less expensive line of jewelry, but she refuses. Because she declines to change the way she views her prospective business, she is stuck in a rut. In the meantime, many other women have launched successful jewelry businesses because they were realistic about the start-up opportunities open to them.

For example, there's Monica Levy. About two years ago, she decided to produce a jewelry line. Up to that point, she had been designing for other companies on a freelance basis and was paid only a fee for her work. If she could manufacture and sell her jewelry herself, her profits would be substantially larger. She, too, was unable to borrow money to launch her business, but she had $10,000 in savings that she could invest. She began by creating a 24-piece collection of sterling silver zodiac earrings and pins that retailed for $35 each. Her samples cost only a dollar or two to produce, so she had plenty of merchandise to present to prospective buyers.

Her first clients have been small jewelry and gift shops in Chicago. Her line is selling so well that she is working on a second collection. She is also hiring sales representatives to expand her market. She will supply them with sample jewelry and promotional materials, and the reps will work on a commission basis. By being realistic about her market and about what she could afford to manufacture, Monica has been able to launch a company with endless possibilities. If she needs to borrow money in the future, her company will have the track record necessary to obtain the funds.

Careful Planning Is the Key to Success

Use this chapter to help decide if you're ready to dive right in. Be careful to consider all of the points discussed here. Analyze your motives and goals. Becoming an entrepreneur may not be the best option for you. If you don't have the skills or experience to launch a new venture, consider working for others, taking courses, seeking business counseling. It can be a very costly mistake to open a business that you aren't prepared to run. And don't forget to analyze your market. If you don't, you're on shaky ground and can end up losing a lot of money. Finally, be flexible. If you have a great idea for a business but can't obtain the start-up funds, alter your plans. Turn your short-term goals into long-term goals. If you really have the entrepreneurial bug, your courage, energy and determination will see you through.

CHAPTER 3

Financing

When You Can't Obtain Bank Financing, Be Creative

$\mathbf{L}$et's begin with the bad news. Start-up companies rarely get bank financing. This is true whether you're a man or a woman, although many of the women I interviewed seemed to think that it's even tougher for them. In fact, a recent study by the Women's Business Development Center in Chicago reported that one of the biggest problems facing women entrepreneurs is access to capital.

So where do women get the funds to launch their businesses? Many borrow on their credit cards or tap their savings and investments. Others ask their family or friends. A few, if they're lucky, have real estate or other collateral they can use to secure a bank loan. How do you decide which is the best option for you? That all depends on the type of business you wish to start, the amount of money you need and your individual circumstances.

Create a Business Plan

Many women feel uncomfortable asking for money to launch a business because they think they won't be taken seriously by bankers or other lenders. The best way to overcome this fear is to take yourself seriously, right from the start, by creating a business plan to help you clarify your needs and define your objectives. Your plan should cover everything from pricing to production, financing to sales. Describe your management team (which may be only you), the background of your company, your product or service, your market and how you will tap it, potential obstacles and ideas for overcoming them. Include information on your company's fiscal needs and explain how you will repay a loan or other financing.

"Everything became concrete for me when I wrote my plan," asserts Arlynn Greenbaum, president of Authors Unlimited, a national lecture bureau that arranges speaking engagements for writers. "I had to deal with all the numbers. How many speakers did I need on my roster to have a critical mass? Where would I find them? How would I market my company? Where would I find customers? Where would I get the start-up money?"

A business plan is essential if you want to approach a bank or venture capitalist for funds. It is also useful if you decide to ask your family or friends for a loan. Although they might lend you money without seeing a business plan, with it, they will know exactly what your business is, why you need money and how you will spend it. A word of caution: If you do borrow from relatives or friends, make sure you have a written agreement stating how much you are borrowing and when you will repay it. Then stick to your payment schedule. This will avoid misunderstandings and keep your friendly lenders from looking over your shoulder.

There are so many books, videotapes and magazine articles explaining how to write a business plan that it's overwhelming trying to choose one. I recommend Geraldine A. Larkin's book, *Woman to Woman* (Prentice Hall, 1993). She devotes a clear and concise chapter to the subject, presenting just enough information to help you get the job done without driving you crazy. Another good book is *Anatomy of a Business Plan,* by Linda Pinson and Jerry Jinnett (Enterprise Dearborn, 1993).

Even if you decide that a formal business plan is not necessary to launch your enterprise, I still advise you to sit down and prepare a simple document for your own use. It should contain a brief description of your company and your market, a list of prospective clients and customers, a budget for the first year and a list of things that you need to do to start your venture.

Starting a Business Without Outside Financing

What happens if you prepare your business plan and you still can't obtain the financing to launch your company? If you're convinced that you have a viable idea, then perhaps, like Arlynn Greenbaum, you'll simply dive right in.

In the spring of 1991, Arlynn decided that time was running out. She wanted to get her business going, with or without a bank loan or the help of outside investors. "There was just no turning back and I knew it. It was like being at the top of an expert ski trail. You're frightened, but you know you can do it. That's how I felt. I had to plunge in, no ifs, ands or buts."

Arlynn realized that she would have to move ahead quickly or she would miss several important deadlines that could make or break her business in the first year. Based on the financial projections she had prepared for investors, she knew that she needed $40,000 to get her business off the ground. Twenty-five thousand of this was needed to produce and mail a catalog, her basic tool for securing speaking engagements for the authors on her roster.

At that point, Arlynn didn't have a roster or any authors on it, but that's how she got her idea for financing. She calculated that if she signed up 150 authors and charged them or their publishers each a nominal fee of $200, she would have $30,000—more than enough to design and print the catalog. The rest of the money would come from her savings account.

Arlynn was relentless in following her plan. Using all of the contacts she had cultivated during a long career in book publishing, she arranged dozens of meetings and within two months signed up her first 150 authors. Since then, she has turned Authors Unlimited into a flourishing lecture bureau representing more than 300 writers who speak to audiences throughout the country. Through it all, Arlynn's courage, energy and determination have been unfailing.

My Own Story—The Launch of Jane Wesman Public Relations

Like Arlynn, I used my own money, plus advances from my clients, to launch my public relations agency in January 1980. And, like Arlynn, I found it a frightening experience at first, but I was ready to take a risk. I was tired of being the publicity director of a big company. I was tired of taking orders.

The first thing I did was prepare a mini–business plan and a budget. I calculated that I would need $3,500 a month for the first year to stay in business. This would cover rent, telephone, postage, electricity, supplies, leased office equipment, transportation and entertainment. I would also need an additional $4,000 to pay for such things as a deposit on office space, furniture, telephone installation and the services of a freelance graphic designer. I did not plan to hire any employees for three to six months. I assumed I could use freelance consultants if necessary.

On top of this, I needed money to live on—to pay for rent, food, medical bills, health club membership, clothes, dry cleaning, etc. I also realized that I would have additional expenses as the year progressed, such as the cost of attending businesses conventions where I hoped to find new clients. Since I had less than $5,000 in my savings account, I knew I would need clients from day one to keep my business going. For several months before I opened my doors, while I was working at my full-time job, I aggressively marketed my new venture during my free time.

On January 2, 1980, I launched Jane Wesman Public Relations with five clients in the fields of art, books and design. I found these clients by phoning, writing and meeting with as many people as possible, using each contact to lead to another.

Each client agreed to pay me at the start of the month for work to be done during the next 30 days. I then continued to bill each client 30 days in advance, and I still do so today. In that way, I can use my clients' money to cover my monthly business expenses.

Many businesses operate in this manner. They insist on receiving some form of payment before the work begins. That's exactly what my landlord does when he sends me a bill at the start of each month. And the same is true of the finance company from which I lease my office equipment. Suppliers of large items, such as custom-made office furniture, also demand an advance payment, usually 50 percent, before they will begin work. Therefore, don't be afraid to ask for some sort of advance payment. It's an accepted business practice.

Creative Ways To Keep Cash Outlays to a Minimum

Over the years, I discovered other ways to obtain funds without having to get a bank loan. For example, when it was time to move to a larger office, I rented space from a landlord who was willing to construct, paint, carpet, light and air-condition the space for me. I made no cash outlay to get the job done, nor did I have to supervise the work. My landlord incorporated the cost of construction into my rent and received a return on his investment during the term of my lease.

Another way to avoid large cash outlays is to lease copier machines, computers and even office furniture. You will pay fairly large amounts of interest, but you can write it all off as a business expense when you file your income taxes. If you buy equipment, the IRS requires you to depreciate it, which may not give you as big a tax write-off at first. Check with your accountant because the tax laws are constantly changing. I lease or buy equipment depending on my cash flow situation at the time I need the item.

For the new entrepreneur, there's another important advantage to leasing office equipment. Unlike applying for a loan for working capital, I had no trouble obtaining credit to lease office equipment right from the start. All I needed was a good personal credit history—in other words, that I used credit cards and department store charge accounts and kept the payments up to date. It didn't matter that my company was a start-up business. My personal credit history sufficed. It's amazing how much you can borrow from banks by obtaining a line of credit or an overdraft on your checking account, or from credit card companies, if you have a good credit record.

Using Collateral To Obtain a Loan

What do you do if you want to launch a company that requires more capital than you have on hand? Nearly 15 years ago, Edith Scott, who was one of the most successful women executives in the home furnishings industry, decided to leave her corporate vice president's job to create a company that manufactures children's furniture. She needed capital to launch her business.

"At first I tried to obtain venture capital," she explains. "And through some miracle, or so I thought, I was able to find it. Then I started to smell a rat." Edith soon realized that in return for the money she would have to give up a large percentage of her business to the venture capitalists, so much so that she would lose control of the company. Instead of having majority ownership of her own company, she would essentially be an employee, just as she was before. She turned down the funding.

Instead, Edith decided to obtain money by mortgaging her vacation home. "I was lucky that I had bought that house while I was still single. In my generation, it was embarrassing for a woman to do well in business, especially well enough to buy a house. Even when I dated, I never told men that I owned it."

But the house has been a godsend for her furniture company. "Several times when we needed cash I used that house as equity to get a loan," Edith says. She points out that many women never consider the fact they may need equity someday. When they get married, their homes are held jointly or in the husband's name, so they can't use the house to obtain capital. "I want to warn women that it's important to own something, especially if you want to start a business. And make sure that whatever it is, it's in your own name."

If You Don't Have Enough Money To Launch Your Ultimate Dream Business, Be Realistic

What if you don't own a home or other form of equity and you still want to launch a business that involves an outlay of capital? My best advice is to think about growing your business in a step-by-step manner. Be realistic about it.

Begin to establish credit early. Use your credit cards for as many purchases as possible, and then pay them off in a timely manner. Take out a small bank loan of perhaps $1,000, but don't spend the money. Use it to pay back the loan. And then borrow again. The credit card company and the bank will report these transactions to TRW or another credit bureau, thus establishing a credit history for you. This will make it easier to obtain a larger loan in the future.

And remember, you can't create a multimillion-dollar company overnight. My first year in business, I paid myself less than $15,000 after expenses. It took many years of long hours and hard work before I could pay myself anything close to what I now make.

What's more, each year wasn't necessarily better than the one before. Sometimes I took a big step forward financially in one year and then a few steps back the next. It was hard not to blame myself for failing to live up to the previous year's income, but I learned that the amount of money I make is not the only measure of my success. Quality of life is extremely important, as is the potential for future success. Sometimes a good year meant that I made less money but developed leads for better projects in the years to come.

Develop a Record of Profitability

No matter what kind of business you want to start, you'll need capital to launch it. If you finance your new venture yourself, make sure you develop and maintain a good credit rating, and keep cash outlays to a minimum. It's easier to obtain a loan later, once your company has a proven record of profitability.

The Future of Financing for Women-Owned Businesses

Organizations such as the Women's Business Development Center and the American Woman's Economic Development Corporation are lobbying to make it easier for women in both new and established companies to obtain financial assistance. And there is hope on the horizon. Many banks, recognizing the economic impact of women-owned businesses, are developing special strategies to help women obtain loans. Meanwhile, the Small Business Administration has taken action with a program to guarantee loans for women entrepreneurs before they approach lenders. I've even read about a private fund that's being developed to invest solely in women-owned businesses. So take a deep breath and dive right in. Build your company and make it profitable. When you need an expansion loan within the next few years, obtaining that capital might be a lot easier than it is today.

CHAPTER 4

Cost, Space, Image and Lifestyle

Working from Home versus Renting an Office

I love working at home. It gives me time and flexibility."
"I hate working at home. I can't get away from my job."
"I love working at home. I don't have to commute."
"I hate working at home. I feel so isolated."

These are some of the comments I received from women entrepreneurs who were asked whether they prefer working at home or in an office. They were adamant about the advantages and disadvantages of each situation. What seemed like a plus to one woman was a drawback to another.

I've always rented an office and would find it difficult to run a business out of my home. To me, running a business means having a professional space—a place where employees can work and clients can visit, a place with plenty of room and a pleasant atmosphere conducive to productivity.

Yet, it's impossible to ignore the way that modern technology has made the home office a viable option for a growing number of women entrepreneurs. Computers, modems, desktop copiers, fax machines and overnight mail have made working from home seem like an ideal situation. But there are drawbacks. For example, working from home can be extremely isolating. It can also inhibit your ability to grow, psychologically as well as physically. Psychologically because working from home lets you avoid the risks of growth. Physically because a lack of space means there's not enough room to add employees. There are some alternatives between working from home and renting your own office. These include sharing space with another small business or renting space in a suite of ready-made offices.

Despite my preference for renting an office, each woman entrepreneur must decide what's right for her. The most important factors to consider are cost, space, image and lifestyle.

Compare the Costs

It costs less to work from home than to pay for office space. Not only do you avoid the extra expense of office rent, but you can deduct a percentage of your home expenses, such as mortgage, rent and utilities, on your tax return. But beware. Before you proceed, check with your accountant. The tax regulations and financial impact of making certain deductions can be very complicated, especially in regard to home mortgages.

What's more, making deductions for a home office sends an immediate signal to the IRS. You stand a better chance of being audited when you claim a home office. Therefore, it's essential to dedicate a specific portion of your home to your office so that you can clearly document your deductions. I can't stress this enough. Whether it's a big closet, an extra bedroom or an entire suite of rooms, use it for business only.

Also check the zoning laws where you live. Some cities and municipalities allow you to work at home; others do not. Don't get caught in a legal quagmire.

And finally, even if you think working at home is the best solution, make an appointment with a real estate agent to see what's available in office space. An office may not cost as much as you imagine, especially since the rent and utilities are completely tax deductible. Although you may decide to launch your business at home, it's always useful to know what type of commercial space is available just in case you decide to expand.

Analyze Your Space Requirements

This is pretty cut and dried—either you have enough space to set up an office at home or you don't. Some women have been able to launch their businesses using a part of the bedroom, dining room or kitchen table. But a minimal amount of space can be uncomfortable, inefficient and extremely frustrating. Any woman who starts this way and who experiences even a modicum of success eventually realizes that she'll either have to find a bigger home or rent a separate office.

If you do opt for a home office and growth is part of your plan, organize your space so that you have room for storage, workstations and employees. If you have a large house, consider creating a separate entrance and lavatory facilities for your employees. This makes a more attractive and productive work environment, and it's more comfortable for you and your family.

Decide What Image You Wish To Project

Although working at home is certainly acceptable in today's business world, it does not always create as professional an image as a separate office does. Ask yourself how you wish to be viewed by your colleagues, clients or customers. Entrepreneurs who work at home are usually considered freelancers or consultants. If this is your niche and projects the right image for you, then stick to a home office. If not, then rent an appropriate space as soon as you can afford one.

Figure Out Your Lifestyle Needs

Lifestyle is probably the most important factor in choosing between working at home or renting an office. If you like to work at odd hours, if you wish to be near your children, if you hate to commute, then working at home may be the solution for you. Some women say they like to roll out of bed in the morning, drink a cup of coffee and get to work while they're still in their pajamas. Others like to work from home because it's easy to take a nap or grab something to eat. They feel more comfortable in their home environment than in an office.

But some women find that working at home can be distracting. There are dishes to wash, closets to rearrange, laundry to do, a dozen things to keep them from getting down to business. The reverse is also true. If they tend to be workaholics, they never find time for personal moments without feeling guilty because their work is staring at them 24 hours a day.

But probably the biggest problem with working at home is a sense of isolation. If you do choose this route, make sure you develop a network of friends and colleagues with whom you can share ideas, problems and solutions.

Making a Home Office a Dream Come True

When Louisville resident Liz Curtis Higgs left her job as a radio disc jockey to launch her speaking career, she was seven months pregnant and wanted to work from home. "A home office is great when you have an infant," she says. "The baby sleeps so much that you have plenty of time to work. It became tougher with the second child. One child was in the crib while the other was into everything else."

For Liz, working at home meant:

- She could see her children during the day.

- Her children knew where she was.

- She saved money on overhead and taxes.

- She did not have to commute.

Once Liz obtained child care, her biggest problem was space. She and her family kept tripping over the boxes of promotional materials that she stored at home. After four years, the floor collapsed from the weight of the boxes. "That's when I decided to rent an office within walking distance of my home," she says.

Although she was no longer tripping over boxes, Liz was never really comfortable in her new office. "The biggest drawback was the fact that I like to work at odd hours. I do a lot of writing, and sometimes the ideas come to me late at night. I'd want to work, but I'd discover that the background information I needed was at the office. I would either have to let the idea go or throw on a raincoat over my pajamas and traipse back to the office. It just didn't work for me."

Despite the obstacles, Liz's business grew by leaps and bounds—she now gives nearly a hundred motivational talks a year—so she and her husband were able to buy a century-old farmhouse with outbuildings on two and a half acres just outside Louisville. "We gutted the outbuildings and had them redesigned as office space. Now my office is just a stone's throw from my home. There's plenty of space for storage and employees. My children are near, but not in my lap. And I can work late at night. I pinch myself each morning when I wake up, delighted that I have the job I've always dreamed of."

On Your Own, But Not Alone: Sharing Space with Another Small Business

One of the most difficult parts of starting a small business is dealing with loneliness. If you're working from home or in a one-person office, it can be difficult to motivate yourself when there's no one to talk to. Sharing space with a another business, whether it's related to yours or not, is a great solution.

Pat Rose of Pat Rose and Associates, a public relations agency in San Francisco, began by working from home. "There's no commute. There's plenty of flextime. You can work in the middle of the night, and you can wear anything you want. Also, there's no one to interrupt you. But it's extremely lonely," she explains. "I had no one to bounce ideas off and I was living in the suburbs. I was too far away from the city."

After a year, Pat found an ideal solution by renting space with two friends, Nancy Crowley and Patsy Barich, who had just become partners in their own public relations agency—Crowley Barich Communications. They now share an office in San Francisco. They split the rent and the cost of the fax machine and copier, but each business has its own telephone system. And since they're in the same field, they can brainstorm as well.

"It's really terrific for moral support and troubleshooting," says Pat. "We're good at critiquing each other's work, and we're very supportive. If one of us doesn't feel well, we encourage her to go home and rest. Otherwise, she probably would stay in the office and work herself ragged."

There are many variations on this idea. You don't have to share space with a company that does exactly the same work as you. The key is to share space with people with whom you feel compatible. I know an art dealer who sublets an office from an architect, a graphic designer who leases space from a small book publisher, and a party planner who uses space in an interior design firm. Each of these women says that although she keeps her business separate from that of her office mate, there is a sense of camaraderie and the sharing of ideas. The other advantage, of course, is a savings in rent and monthly expenses such as utilities.

Creating a Professional Image for Less: Renting a Ready-Made Office

"Office suites" or shared office spaces have sprung up in metropolitan areas across the country, providing an economical alternative for entrepreneurs who want the prestige of a business office at a lower cost.

Arlynn Greenbaum of Authors Unlimited took advantage of such a setup when she launched her company, because she wanted to project a professional image without making a large cash outlay for office equipment and rent. After doing some research, she found a landlord who had divided a floor of an office building into separate, small offices that could be rented on a monthly or annual basis. All the businesses share the entry, reception area, receptionist and conference rooms. They also have copier and fax machine privileges. Telephones, which connect through a central switchboard, are installed in each office.

"This is an incredibly low-cost way to rent an office," Arlynn points out. "All I had to buy when I started out was a computer. Everything else was already provided. And as my company grows, I can obtain more space within the complex without having to change my stationery or telephone number."

Successful Leasing Strategies

If you decide to lease your own office or retail space, use a good real estate agent, one who is familiar with the market for your type of space. A knowledgeable agent can locate space that's not commonly advertised and may even be able to help you negotiate a more favorable lease. The agent's fee is generally paid by the landlord. Ask about this before you start working together. Remember, though, a real estate agent is not a lawyer. Never sign a lease that you don't understand and that you haven't reviewed with your lawyer.

When looking for space, the things to consider are location, amenities and rent.

Location

In choosing a location for my office, I was mainly concerned about finding a space that was centrally located and near public transportation to make it convenient for my employees and clients to reach. If you work in an area where people will be driving to your office, try to lease a space close to a main thoroughfare or highway and make sure there's plenty of parking.

If you're opening a retail business, there are several other things you should know about location. You don't want to open a store in an isolated area, nor do you want to open up on a street where the competition is so great that you'll be run out of business. Choose an affordable area with a reasonable amount of customer traffic.

Pamela Welsh had a large collection of antique furniture that she wanted to sell, so she rented a loft in a professional building in New York City and opened up shop. There were no other furniture showrooms in the building, but she had excellent contacts in the interior design field and thought people would go out of their way to see her. Unfortunately, she was wrong. After struggling for a year, she moved her business to a street-level store near other upscale furniture shops. Although her rent was higher, customer traffic and sales increased as well. The trick, she learned, is leasing space at a good price in an appropriate location. Balancing location and cost is essential. You don't want your rent to obliterate your profits.

Amenities

I was also concerned about amenities when I leased my office. I wanted to be in a building that was well run with a good staff and superintendent. A handsome lobby, clean hallways and bathrooms, central air-conditioning, daily trash collection and 24-hour access and security were important considerations, and I wanted it all at a reasonable, fair market rent. I decided to forego a fancy address to be able to afford these amenities in an office with enough space so that all of my employees could have private offices. We also have plenty of room for meetings and for storage.

The Lease

Before you sign a lease, read it carefully. Then show it to your lawyer. Some commercial leases are extremely complicated and include large escalation clauses tied to tax increases and building staff wages. Take the time to understand what you're getting into, and make sure you'll be able to cover the additional costs. If a lease agreement seems unreasonable, don't sign it. Find another space.

Avoid Escalation Clauses

Kerrie Buitrago of Pierrot advises, "Try to negotiate a lease based on a straight monthly rent. When we signed the lease for our pastry shop, it included an escalation clause pegged to gross receipts. That nearly killed us." For years, Kerrie had to pay her landlord additional rent based on the gross income of her business. Even when she did not make a profit, because her expenses were greater than her income, she had to pay the extra rent.

"Walk away from any lease that doesn't suit you," she advises. "We signed the lease for our pastry shop because our emotions overcame our better judgment. We convinced ourselves that if we didn't sign that lease we would never find a suitable space for our shop. But that's nonsense. There's always a space available if you look hard enough."

Review the Lease When You Renew

When you're new in business and signing a lease for the first time, you probably won't have much bargaining power with your landlord. But each time the lease comes up for renewal you'll be in a stronger position, especially if you've turned out to be a desirable tenant (i.e., someone who pays the rent on time). Make sure you review the lease carefully at renewal. You can ask for new concessions or try to remove troublesome clauses.

Sheila Anderson renewed the lease for her clothing store three times without reviewing it. That was a terrible mistake, because her husband had personally guaranteed the rent on the original lease when her business was young. By the third time she renewed, she had been paying rent for 12 years. By then, a personal guarantee from her spouse should not have been necessary.

This would not have been a problem, except that in 1990 the retail clothing business was decimated by the recession. Sheila was paying an exorbitant rent and could barely make enough in sales to keep her store afloat. She was desperate to close her shop, but the landlord refused to cancel her lease, knowing that her husband was legally responsible for the rent. For two years, Sheila worked like a dog just to break even. "It was agony. The day that lease finally expired was one of the happiest moments of my life," she recalls.

Choose Carefully

Whether you decide to work at home or in an office, each option has its advantages and disadvantages. It's up to you to choose the one that suits you best. If working at home seems like the right solution, then try it. You can always move to a separate office at a future time. If you want to start right out with a professional office but are worried about overextending yourself, try sharing space or subletting a small office from another firm. Another viable option is renting space in a group of ready-made office suites. Whether you are renting an office or retail shop, choose a suitable location and avoid signing a lease that contains unfavorable terms. Finding the right place for your business can enhance your ability to succeed. Make your choice wisely.

CHAPTER 5

Choosing the Right Accountant and Lawyer

In general, no business can run smoothly without the services of a qualified accountant. And, as much as we like to joke about the members of the legal profession, a good lawyer is an invaluable asset to any small business. Choosing the wrong professional can be a costly emotional, financial and time-consuming error. Some women business owners make the mistake of hiring a friend or the first accountant or lawyer they meet without ascertaining whether he or she is the best fit for their business. And then, if things go wrong, they procrastinate or feel paralyzed about finding a replacement.

The problem is not knowing what to expect. What can an accountant do for you? Why and when do you need a lawyer? How can you judge the work they do on your behalf? Another problem, which is especially true of fledgling business owners, is feeling intimidated when you interview a prospective lawyer or accountant. At a time when you're particularly vulnerable, when you're not certain whether your business will succeed, it's easy to imagine that the prospective accountant or lawyer is not going to take you seriously as a client, especially if you're a woman. And so, instead of conducting an interview, you end up trying to impress someone.

Know What You Need and What To Expect

The first two steps in your search for the right professional are analyzing your needs and then understanding what a lawyer or accountant can do for you. For most small businesses, an accountant is someone who will work with you throughout the year, while a lawyer is generally needed only at the start of the business to set up the legal structure and create basic contracts. You would then contact your lawyer as necessary when problems or questions arise.

Although I speak with my accountant often, I can go for long stretches without consulting my lawyer. Having an ongoing relationship with a lawyer who knows my business, though, is invaluable. If someone asks me to sign a new or unusual contract, I can send it to my lawyer for review. Or if I find myself in a sticky business situation, I have a good lawyer on my side. It gives me confidence to know that I don't have to search for counsel when the going gets rough.

Lawyers and accountants are there to advise you, but it is not their job to make the final business decision. It's up to you to have the courage and foresight to figure out what to do after getting their input. It's useless to feel frustrated or betrayed if they can't tell you in absolute terms how you should handle a difficult situation. In fact, a negative mind-set can make the decision-making process that much harder because it keeps you from listening to and understanding your advisers' counsel.

It's also a mistake to blame your lawyer or accountant when business is off. It is not their responsibility to run your company for you or to find you new business. So what can you expect of them? Following is a list of the things accountants and lawyers can do to help you.

An accountant can:

- Give you an overall picture of the tax codes and requirements that affect your business.

- File the proper forms so that the government knows you are starting a business.

- Obtain an employer identification number for you.

- Advise you on your business and personal taxes.

- Explain the tax advantages of incorporating or forming a sole proprietorship or partnership. (If you incorporate or form a partnership, your lawyer would then file the proper papers. In most states, it's fairly easy to file the papers for a sole proprietorship yourself.)

- Help you create an efficient bookkeeping system.

- Help you decide whether to write checks manually or by computer. If by computer, your accountant can help you choose a software program and get it running.

- Prepare all appropriate returns for income tax, sales tax, payroll taxes, etc.

- Explain the basic differences between various retirement plans, such as IRAs, SEP-IRAs, Keoghs and 401(k) plans. (Some accountants will suggest that you speak with a pension expert before going further.)

- Advise you about the tax benefits of making certain business decisions, such as leasing or buying office equipment.

- Prepare monthly or quarterly income reports showing how much money you've made and how much you've spent.

- Represent you during a tax audit.

A lawyer can:

- Give you an overall view of the laws concerning your business.

- Explain the legal ramifications of incorporating as opposed to creating a partnership or sole proprietorship.

- Prepare and file the forms to incorporate your business, if that is the business structure you choose.

- Review contracts, such as your office lease or suppliers' contracts, before you sign them.

- Prepare the basic contracts for use with clients or customers.

- Advise you on your obligations as an employer and prepare employment contracts for you.

- Serve as an adviser when you have questions involving clients, competitors or employees.

- Represent you in contract negotiations.

- Help you take legal action to enforce a contract or collect money.

- Represent you in a lawsuit or threatened lawsuit.

Where To Look for an Accountant or a Lawyer

There are a few common-sense rules to follow in hiring an accountant or lawyer. First and foremost, look for a professional who specializes in small businesses. According to CPA Jay Goldstein, "The worst thing you can do is hire a friend who's the comptroller of a big corporation to do your taxes. He may be an expert at profit-and-loss calculations, but he probably won't know all the tax forms that small businesses must file. Find an accountant who is familiar with the needs of small business—someone who is up to date on current tax laws as they affect small businesses." The same is true of a lawyer. An attorney who specializes in international or matrimonial law is not the right choice for your small business.

Seek Recommendations

The best way to find an accountant or lawyer is to ask for recommendations from other small-business owners whose judgment you trust. Make sure that they have worked with the person and have been satisfied with the services rendered.

Tap Your Network

Another way to look for a professional is through networking, social introductions or word of mouth. In these cases, you probably won't have the benefit of being introduced by someone who has worked with the accountant or lawyer. If you are serious about working with the person, see if you can speak to one or two of the firm's other clients to get a recommendation.

Pay Attention to Articles and Speeches

You might also find a prospective accountant or lawyer through an article, speech, direct-mail piece or advertisement prepared by the accounting or law firm. Again, it's wise to obtain a recommendation from another client before making your final decision. (I usually shy away from lawyers or accountants who advertise their services to a general audience, but if the ad is directed towards your type of business, it might be worthwhile to follow up.)

Narrowing the Field

It's important to interview several professionals before making your final decision. You will get a better picture of who's available and the types of services they provide. I recently spoke with the owner of a small retail shop in Baltimore who has been in business for a decade and has worked with the same accountant from the start. He was the only one she ever interviewed. She says he's dependable when it comes to preparing and filing tax returns, but, she adds, "I don't feel in control of my earnings and expenses. I believe business is good, but I don't know why I don't have more money. When I ask my accountant to talk with me about what's happening, he refuses."

As we explored her problem, we discovered that her accountant was not providing her with computerized profit-and-loss reports that delineate income and expenses and make comparisons to previous quarters or years. She had no idea that such reports were available and that they would help her understand how she was spending her money. She agreed to ask her accountant for reports and, if he refused, to look for someone else.

A woman who runs a graphic design studio told me that she is also unhappy with her accountant but won't let him go because "he's cheap." If she had done some comparison shopping, she would have discovered that his fees are comparable to those of other small accounting firms. She could certainly afford to switch.

Don't Be Bamboozled by a Smooth Talker

I had plenty of problems, too, when I hired my first accountant. In the beginning, I was overwhelmed by the idea of taxes—not just income taxes, but corporate taxes, Social Security taxes, unemployment insurance taxes and, in New York City, commercial rent tax. I was terrified that I would overlook something and end up owing thousands of dollars in penalties and fines.

Although I was desperate to find an accountant, I didn't know how to conduct a proper search. At a party one evening, a friend gave me the name and number of Joe, his former accountant. My friend said that although he didn't get along with Joe, I probably would. This comment should have stopped me from going any further, but it didn't.

I called and made an appointment. Joe was a real smooth talker. I was mesmerized by his confident air and his good looks, and I was too naive to interview anyone else.

Joe assured me that he could take care of all my accounting needs. So, for the next year, I'd traipse up to his office every quarter with my check stubs, canceled checks and bank statements under my arm. I'd leave them for a week or so while Joe's bookkeeper compiled, by hand, huge ledger sheets of income and expenses that were completely useless to me. Like every other small-business owner, I needed a profit-and-loss report. I also needed to keep my records in my own office. Each time I left them at Joe's, I felt my business was being held hostage, since it was impossible for me to make spending decisions without my checkbook.

Whenever I asked if there was a better way to handle the bookkeeping, Joe said I was being "silly" for questioning his procedures. He was also expensive, hard to reach by phone and took forever to prepare my tax returns.

The situation might have continued indefinitely if he hadn't made a careless mistake computing my quarterly withholding taxes, which led to a big penalty. I was furious, but I suddenly saw the light. This accountant was a jerk. I had trusted him for over a year because he was a smooth talker and I was too scared or too naive to look elsewhere. So I fired him.

This experience showed me what I needed from an accountant. I wanted someone who knew the tax codes inside and out, who would answer my questions when I telephoned him, who would come to my office to balance the books, who would send me computerized reports and who would prepare my tax returns in a timely manner.

After interviewing several accountants, I found the perfect one. Not only does he do a great job, but he charges me half of what Joe did.

Ask Key Questions before Hiring a Professional

When you interview a prospective accountant or attorney, be sure to get straight answers to your questions. If you find the answers difficult to understand, or if the candidate is not forthcoming, look for someone else.

Try to raise the following questions when interviewing an accountant:

1. Are you a certified public accountant? (In choosing between a CPA and a noncertified accountant, find out whether you will need accountant's reports for such things as bank loans or to interest prospective investors. Each state has different rules, but only a CPA can prepare certified statements that may be necessary to obtain loans, credit, a business partner or an investor. Also, in order to become a CPA, an accountant must pass a special examination and take a certain number of professional continuing education courses each year.)

2. Do you concentrate on working with small businesses? (It's essential to find an accountant who does.)

3. How do you stay current on the latest tax laws and regulations? (My accountant attends classes and seminars on a regular basis. He also has an entire tax library, including research material and tax forms, on CD-ROM, making it easy for him to answer difficult tax questions in a matter of minutes. It's important that your accountant be computerized.)

4. Have you handled any IRS or other tax audits? How did you do?

5. Will I be working directly with you or with someone else in your firm? (If you will be working with someone else, ask to meet him or her.)

6. How do you propose that we work together? Do you handle the bookkeeping or do I? (You will save a con-

siderable amount of money if you handle the bookkeeping yourself. You, an employee or a part-time bookkeeper can do such tasks as writing checks and balancing the checkbook. According to Jay Goldstein, "It's important for business owners to keep thorough records of income and expenses." This makes an accountant's job more efficient and less expensive for you. If you need help, read *Keeping the Books,* by Linda Pinson and Jerry Jinnett (Upstart, 1993).

7. Will you help me organize a bookkeeping system?

8. What type of profit-and-loss reports will you prepare for me, and how often? What information will they include? Will you help me analyze them? (Most small businesses need quarterly profit-and-loss statements. Ask how the statements will be customized to fit your needs.)

9. How do you bill for your services? And how often do you bill? (Try to arrange for an annual fee, to be paid in installments, so you know in advance what your costs will be. In addition to the fee, most accountants charge extra to handle tax audits.)

The following questions will be helpful in selecting a lawyer:

1. What is the nature of your law practice?

2. Do you represent other small-business owners? (This is essential. A lawyer needs to understand the problems a small business faces. For example, if you want your lawyer to prepare a standard contract for your clients, the contract needs to be simple and easy to understand. After spending weeks negotiating a deal, the last thing you want is to send the new client a contract that is so complicated he or she refuses to sign it.)

3. Have you ever represented anyone in my business or profession? (This is helpful because it means the lawyer will be familiar with the dynamics of your business.)

4. May I see a list of representative clients? May I call any for references?

5. Do you bill for your services at an hourly rate or as a flat fee? How much and how often do you bill? (If the lawyer charges by the hour, ask for an estimate of the amount of time it will take to handle your specific needs. Also ask to be billed monthly instead of bimonthly or quarterly. It's easier to ask about the specifics of a monthly bill and to stop your lawyer from doing unnecessary work if you change your business strategy or have underestimated the cost of the lawyer's services. Remember that if you seek help for a specific problem during the preliminary interview, you may be billed for the lawyer's time. Ask about this before you make your initial appointment.)

6. Will you or a colleague be handling my work or my requests for counsel? (If you will be working with someone else, ask to meet that person.)

You should then ask a few questions about issues or problems the lawyer may have to handle on your behalf. See how he or she responds and whether you feel comfortable with this viewpoint. Some lawyers are very aggressive and always ready to take legal action to solve a problem, while others would rather negotiate a solution. I prefer the latter because lawsuits are costly, time-consuming and emotionally draining, although sometimes the mere filing of a lawsuit may provide the necessary leverage to negotiate a good settlement.

Don Savelson, an attorney with Proskauer, Rose, Goetz, and Mendelsohn, says, "Document, document, document. Put as much in writing as possible. Written documents provide stronger evidence than oral testimony and make it easier for a lawyer to analyze your problem and assess your ability to prevail." He also advises clients to treat their lawyers like their doctors. Don't hold back any information. It may have a damaging effect later in a case.

To help save time and money, Savelson also suggests that you put your ideas on paper before visiting your lawyer. "If you need to have a contract prepared, make a list of the points you want covered and send it to your lawyer before he or she begins working on it. That way, your attorney won't have to spend as much time drawing out information from you during a meeting or telephone conversation. If you're paying by the hour, this can be a big savings."

Three Lawyers Can Give You Three Different Opinions

Several years ago, Marsha Gold, head of a small company that creates parties and special events, had trouble with a former employee. The employee had quit and started a company to go head to head with Marsha. "I didn't mind the competition," explains Marsha. "What bothered me was that she took all of my client mailing lists and was using them to find new business. What's more, she was sending out letters implying that she, not my firm, had organized dozens of important parties and other well-publicized events. Some of my clients started calling me and asking what was going on."

Marsha wanted to take legal action, so she interviewed three attorneys. The first one immediately told her to sue her former employee for all she was worth. The attorney's fee would be at least $25,000. Marsha felt it wasn't worth the money.

The second lawyer wanted to avoid a lawsuit but suggested sending a threatening letter to the former employee. The attorney outlined the type of demands she would make. Marsha felt that this approach was too harsh.

The third lawyer suggested that instead of spending money on legal fees, Marsha intensify her marketing efforts to compete for new clients. In the meantime, the attorney would write to Marsha's former employee to try to retrieve the mailing lists and to ask her to stop disseminating misleading information. He would also prepare a contract which Marsha could ask future employees to sign that would limit their ability to compete directly with her for a reasonable amount of time after their departure. Marsha decided that he was the right attorney for her. She has continued to seek his counsel ever since.

Checklist for Hiring a Professional

If you need the services of an accountant, lawyer, graphic designer, pension expert, marketing consultant or other outside adviser, remember to:

- Analyze your needs.

- Know what to expect.

- Ask for recommendations from people whose judgment you trust.

- Interview several prospective candidates.

- Hire the consultant or professional with whom you feel most comfortable.

- If there's a problem after you start working together, don't be afraid to let the professional know that you're dissatisfied. Be polite but direct about what you expect.

- If things don't change after a reasonable amount of time, find someone else. Don't be deceived by a smooth-talking pro.

CHAPTER 6

Hiring the Right Employees

Learning to hire the right people seems like a lifelong task. After nearly 25 years of hiring employees, both as a corporate executive and as a business owner, I think I've finally gotten it right. Along the way, though, I've made some mistakes, hiring the wrong people for all kinds of well-meaning but misguided reasons, such as:

- Feeling sorry for someone who begged me for just one chance.

- Liking a person's sense of humor and imagining she'd be fun to have around.

- Wanting to nurture a lost soul.

- Thinking I couldn't afford anyone better.

I've hired people whom I thought were perfect for the job only to discover that I didn't really listen to them during the interviewing process. I've hired others because I liked the way they looked and I thought they would impress my clients. My biggest mistake was hiring someone I thought was qualified for the job but who really did not have enough experience. I'm not alone in finding the hiring process difficult. Making good choices takes practice. If you don't get it right at first, don't blame yourself; just keep trying.

Why Do I Need Employees?

The most important reason to have employees is to help you make more money. Without employees, you have to handle everything yourself, from the simplest chores such as ordering office supplies to the most complex ones such as negotiating contracts. Employees give you the time to focus on the critical tasks that generate the most income for your business. They also give you the time to think about your business, to be creative and to develop new strategies.

Yet many women, particularly those who work as freelancers or consultants, are fearful of putting anyone on their payroll. Their reasons usually fall into four categories:

1. I don't want the headache of being responsible for someone else.

2. I can't find anyone who can do the job well enough.

3. By the time I show someone how to do the job, I could get it done myself.

4. I can't afford an employee.

The first three reasons for not hiring employees are excuses, not business decisions. Don't let your fears stand in the way of doing something that will help you succeed. As for the fourth point, if you are not generating enough income to hire an employee, you may have to pass. But remember that having someone help you, even if it's only part-time, will allow your business to grow. Without employees, you limit your possibilities for success. Look at the big picture. If you are content with your business the way it is, then employees don't matter. But if you are interested in running a larger or more complex operation, then you'll need help.

Think about hiring employees the same way you would think about adding a computer or upgrading your telephone system. Will the investment help you make more money by enhancing sales, increasing efficiency or allowing you to produce more work? Remember, you don't have to make the whole investment at once. If you hire someone for $20,000 a year, you'll pay the person's salary in weekly installments as you generate income. If after a reasonable trial you discover that you hired the wrong person, you can let the employee go. If this happens, don't kick yourself; just look for a replacement. If you think there may be a legal problem in firing someone, check with your attorney before you hire or during employment, not after termination.

Hiring Your First Employee Takes the Most Courage

Anita Anderson came to me last year with a business problem. She ran her consulting firm from home without any support staff. Since she had more work than she could handle, she split many of her jobs with two other freelancers, giving them as much as 50 percent of her fees. Unfortunately, she often had to redo their work, so she had trouble making a profit.

I suggested that Anita try to handle most of the jobs herself with the help of one or two employees. Whatever remained could be contracted out. I saw the following advantages:

- She would make more money by not having to give away half of each fee.

- She could train employees who would be loyal and who could eventually take on more complicated tasks.

- She would have people to brainstorm with.

- She would have more free time to look for new business because her employees could handle the less important tasks for her. Thus, her business would grow.

To begin, I suggested she hire one assistant to handle simple chores such as answering the phone, typing, copying and updating mailing lists. But Anita was terrified of making the commitment. She had a dozen excuses for continuing as she was. She was convinced that no one would want to work in a small home-based office. But her biggest fear was financial. With outside consultants, she was not responsible for payroll taxes, health insurance, sick pay or supplies. I pointed out that as soon as she eliminated the freelancers she would have more than enough to hire an assistant and make a profit on each job. She would also save herself a lot of emotional suffering. When Anita finally took the plunge and ran a "Help Wanted" ad, she was pleasantly surprised by the number of resumes she received.

It took her about six weeks to review the resumes, interview applicants and find the right person. Since then, her profits have increased by nearly 30 percent, her stress level has been reduced, and she's now looking for her second assistant.

Secrets of Successful Hiring

Patrice Tanaka, CEO and creative director of P.T.&Co., a New York firm that's known as a great place to work, says, "Of everything I do, hiring requires the most care. There are many qualified people out there, but finding the one who is absolutely right for us takes a great deal of hard work."

Patrice's company employs nearly two dozen people. "We want people to feel secure in their jobs. It's bad for morale when you have a lot of turnover, so we try hard to find the right people." Hiring is an ongoing process at her firm. She wants to know who is available at all times in case she has a sudden opening. Therefore, she is very responsive to people who send her unsolicited but interesting resumes or who are recommended by colleagues, suppliers or friends. She interviews nearly 50 people a year, whether or not she has a job opening at the moment.

Patrice believes that there's an added benefit to spending so much time interviewing prospective employees. "It's good word of mouth. It gives people a chance to see what we're doing and to spread the word." She has even found new clients this way. "Someone I interviewed got a job in the public relations department of a big consumer goods company. When the company needed a new public relations agency, my contact recommended us and we signed the account."

Patrice also tries to create a work environment that is comfortable and supportive, yet challenging and dynamic. "I don't want people to work here just for the money, because they'll leave as soon as another company offers them more. People have to want to work for us because we offer more in quality-of-life benefits." Some of the benefits at P.T.&Co. include flexible work schedules, a relaxed dress policy, generous maternity benefits and incentives for all employees to participate in new business development.

If you're hiring your first employee, you probably can't offer as much as Patrice, but do consider such perks as flexible working hours or a generous vacation policy. If necessary, let someone work from home one day a week. These are things that people really value and that make them better employees.

Know What You're Looking For

No matter what stage you're at in your business, you need to know what you're looking for before you hire an employee. Women sometimes make the mistake of hiring with their hearts instead of their heads. If they like someone, qualified or not, they figure they can mold the job to fit the person. Although it's good to be flexible, you need to hire someone who fits the job.

The best way to ensure that the person fits the job is to prepare a thorough, written job description. Be specific. What does the job entail? Answering the telephone? Opening the mail? Creating correspondence? Selling new products? Bookkeeping? Managing outside suppliers?

What skills does the employee need? A good telephone manner? Organizational abilities? Computer skills? Strong sales ability? Knowledge of a foreign language? Good industry contacts? Specific technical skills?

Then ask yourself how much experience someone needs to do the job well. Do you want an entry-level person or an experienced pro? Will you have time to train, or do you want someone to walk in and get right to work? Put all this information in writing so that you can ask appropriate questions during the interviewing process.

Where To Look for Prospective Employees

When I need a new employee, I generally run an ad in the "Help Wanted" section of the newspaper. Although I have found this an excellent way to attract applicants, some of my colleagues say ads don't work for them.

The trick is to place the ad under the correct heading in the classified section and to use an intriguing headline. Classified ads are sold by size. Let's assume you can afford a three-inch ad. Don't fill the space with a lot of verbiage describing the job. Instead, think about what makes the job unique and interesting, and try to express this in a catchy headline. Then, in the body of the ad, list the job requirements.

I've discovered that if I run an ad in the "Public Relations" section of the classifieds, using a standard headline that describes the position, such as "Administrative Assistant" or "Account Executive," I receive dozens of resumes from unqualified people. But if I use a headline such as "Books, Art, Culture" to describe my firm's specialties, I get a much higher response from applicants who are experienced in these areas of public relations.

Always end the ad by asking applicants to send their resumes and salary requirements. This is a quick way to ascertain what the going salary is for a particular position. And always include your company name and address, not a box number. You're asking applicants to trust you with their resumes. They deserve to know who's reading them. I believe this encourages a greater response.

In addition to running classified ads, use your network of contacts. Ask other people in your field if they can recommend someone to fill the job. Ask your suppliers, clients and customers. Call your colleagues. If the job is for an intern or a beginner, call the placement office of your local college or university. If you need someone with more experience, run an ad in your professional association's newsletter.

If none of this works, you might try using an employment agency. "A good agency will screen perhaps twenty or twenty-five people, and then send you the three or four who are truly qualified for your job," explains Susan Gordon, president of the Lynn Palmer Agency. "Then it's up to you to choose the one you like the best."

But this can be expensive for a small business. According to Susan, agencies generally charge a commission of 1 percent per $1,000 of the first year's salary, to be paid either by the employer or the employee. Therefore, if you hire someone for $20,000, the commission will be $4,000, or 20 percent of $20,000. Susan says that most agencies put a cap on commissions at 30 percent. (I would advise against asking an employee to pay this fee, because it's not a generous way to start a working relationship.)

Selecting Candidates To Interview

If you do the job search yourself, once you start receiving resumes, use your written job description to choose the best candidates. Call them first so that you can interview them briefly over the phone. You may decide to eliminate some based on the initial telephone conversation.

I usually interview ten to twelve candidates for a high-level position. If I'm seeking a college student for a part-time job, then my office manager does the interviewing. After screening students by phone, she asks three or four to come in for an interview. We find that for entry-level positions it's time-consuming and confusing to interview too many applicants, because most of them have little or no job experience. We are looking for someone with a quick mind and an upbeat personality who will work hard and ask the right questions.

The Job Interview: Listen, Listen, Listen

What you ask during an interview is not nearly as important as how you listen. Don't get carried away talking about yourself and your business. Don't glamorize or apologize for your company. Instead, make the applicant feel welcome. Give a brief description of the job and what your company does, and then begin asking questions.

To make the interview run more smoothly, I usually give applicants information about my company as soon as they arrive. I then wait about ten minutes to give them time to scan the material. If an applicant chooses not to read the information, I assume that he or she is not the right candidate.

After a brief welcome, I ask applicants about their work experience. I encourage them to be as specific as possible by reviewing their resumes with them, asking for details about each of their former positions. I ask how their jobs were structured and how much responsibility they had. I then ask them to describe their most successful projects and their most difficult ones. I also ask to see samples of their work. Then comes the key question. I describe a situation or a project for which they would be responsible and ask them what they would do. It's more important to me to know how they would handle a project in my office than how they handled something in the past. It's essential to be relaxed. Don't intimidate a prospective employee during an interview if you want to get the most out of him or her.

What To Look For

Julie Lewit-Nirenberg of *Mademoiselle* magazine says, "When I interview, I look for presence and intelligence. I want to find out how people think strategically. For sales reps, I want to know what was their toughest sell? How did they get around objections? I want to hire someone I'd like to buy from. If the person makes me feel uncomfortable, then they're not right for me."

Patrice Tanaka says that she, too, looks for intelligence. She also looks for "creativity, resourcefulness, a sense of humor, a generosity of spirit, a healthy sense of competitiveness and an obsessive-compulsive streak that tells me he or she will persevere until the desired result is achieved."

Making the Final Choice

After completing the initial round of interviews, I usually ask the four or five best applicants to come back a second time. Generally, the applicant is a bit more relaxed during a second interview, and it gives me a chance to see if I still perceive him or her in the same way. I ask myself, Is this the person I want to see in my office tomorrow morning? The person who can take the ball and run with it? The person who has enough experience to do what is required—who will work well with the rest of the staff and be a good addition to our team? I often realize during this second interview that the applicant is not as qualified as I had originally thought.

I then narrow the field to two or three candidates who meet with other members of my staff. Afterward, if my staff has strong reactions, either positive or negative, I listen carefully. It's important in a small company to create a harmonious relationship among employees. In the end, though, I always make the final choice.

Negotiating Salary

I believe that you get what you pay for in this world, as long as you don't throw your money around foolishly. When you pay employees fairly, you usually get good work in return. With a new employee, problem one is calculating how much the job is worth. Problem two is negotiating. Problem three is making sure the new employee realizes you are offering a fair salary.

Problem One: Here are a few points I consider when calculating salaries for new employees:

- Going rate. I try to be competitive with other small companies in the field.

- Ability to pay. I try to project income and expenses for the year, including salaries. I want to make sure I will have enough cash flow each week to meet payroll. The fastest way to lose employees is not to pay them on time, even if you're only a few days late. It destroys their sense of confidence.

- Ability to give raises. Since I expect employees to stay with my firm for several years, I want to make sure I'll be able to give them annual raises. This means that I start them off a bit lower than they may like so that their salaries have room to grow.

Problem Two: If I wish to hire someone who wants more than I can afford (or feel comfortable paying), I usually negotiate the following:

- A job and salary review after six months. I explain, though, that a raise is not guaranteed.

- A bonus at the end of the year tied to the employee's performance and the firm's annual sales. Bonuses are an excellent way to recognize a job well done without having to increase the employee's salary.

- Flexible working hours or additional vacation days. Since many of my employees are working mothers, this is usually a valuable perk for them.

- Health insurance. Although I automatically provide health insurance for each employee after three months, I sometimes use this as a negotiating point and let the prospective employee know how much health insurance is worth. Since employees don't pay income taxes on this benefit, it's actually worth more to them than the face amount. It's also advantageous to me because I don't pay payroll taxes on health insurance.

Problem Three: The key to negotiating with new employees is to make sure that they know you appreciate their talents and their skills and that you are offering them a fair salary. If the offer is lower than they want, do not apologize or make excuses. The worst thing you can say is that business is bad. No one wants to join a firm that is having financial difficulties.

Be positive about the job and the opportunities it provides. You can be somewhat flexible about your salary offer, but don't break the bank just because you think you have found the perfect employee.

If someone turns you down because of money, he or she probably was not the right person, at least not at the moment. Stay in touch for future employment, but in the meantime, keep looking. There's someone else out there who is perfect for your company. Employees give you the opportunity to grow your business. They enhance the work experience by being there to help and support you. It's worth the effort to find the right ones.

CHAPTER 7

Motivating Your Staff for Peak Performance

Like hiring, learning to motivate employees takes time and experience, especially for a small-business owner. When I started my company, I assumed that motivating my staff would be no different than it was when I worked as a corporate executive. How wrong I was.

As a corporate executive, I was part of an established hierarchy. There were rules about who reported to whom, about when people received raises and promotions, about hiring and firing, about salaries and benefits. My staff and I were part of a bigger organization, so there were plenty of other people to turn to for help. What's more, someone else was paying my staff. I didn't have to find the money every week to cover their salaries.

When I hired my first employee at Jane Wesman Public Relations, everything was different. It was just the two of us in tight quarters. I had been in business for about six months, and it was hard to hide my anxieties about launching a new company, about finding new clients, about paying the bills. I tended to magnify small problems and I lost my temper unnecessarily. But I also shared each triumph and success.

It's to the credit of my first employee, Lori Ames Stuart, that after working for me for three years and then leaving to take a high-level position elsewhere for the next six, she returned in 1991 to take over as vice president of my firm. When I asked her recently what she thinks I do to motivate employees, she replied, "You don't do anything to motivate us—we love working here." Her spontaneous response showed me that I have indeed come a long way if motivating my staff seems so natural that no one knows I'm doing it. The truth is, I've worked hard at learning how to treat employees so that they are happy and productive.

Motivation begins with the job interview. If you hire the wrong person, you will never be able to motivate him or her, no matter how hard you try. Communicating, training and creating a good work environment are other key motivators.

Ten Ways To Inspire Your Staff

1. Communicate. Make sure your employees know what you expect of them. Describe the job and your expectations before hiring, and reiterate your expectations regularly. With a new employee, this may be a daily necessity. Later, it can be done weekly. Be specific. For example, don't say, "I want you to double your sales this month." Explain how you expect someone to do so, perhaps by changing the sales pitch, developing a new client list or making more sales call per day.

2. Train. Take the time to train your employees in your ways of doing business. It may be time-consuming in the beginning, but it will pay off. And remember that no matter how much time you think it will take to train

someone, it will probably take longer, even with experienced employees. Last year, I hired a senior publicist. I assumed it would take her about four weeks to familiarize herself with our projects, learn our methods and take on a full workload. Eight weeks later, she was still having trouble meeting deadlines. I was becoming frustrated and felt I was spending too much time training her. She claimed I was being impatient.

Neither one of us was willing to give up, though. We set a deadline of four more weeks, by which time she believed she would be able to work independently. During the four-week trial period, I continued to work closely with her, giving her all the advice and feedback she requested. She, in return, put in extra hours and made a special effort to get all of her projects under control. In the end, everything worked out well. It was certainly worth the extra time it took to train this employee. She is now an invaluable addition to my staff.

3. Recognize that people want to do a good job. They do not make mistakes because they think it's fun, or because they want to spite you or make you lose money. I've seen business owners scream in rage over employees' mistakes as if they were made on purpose.

4. Give employees honest and direct feedback. Don't wait until you're ready to explode to tell someone that the job is not being done right. The reverse is also true. I encourage my staff to tell me early on if they see a problem with a project or assignment. In this way, we look for a solution before it's too late.

5. Let employees know that you appreciate their contributions to your company. Make them feel that what they do is important to you and makes a difference to the company. This includes everyone, right down to the receptionist, who needs to know that the way he or she

deals with people on the telephone or visitors to the office is vital in establishing a courteous and professional image for the company.

6. Eliminate fear. Be honest and accessible. Don't play favorites. And don't tolerate abusive behavior from anyone—suppliers, clients or employees. If in doubt about how to treat an employee, ask yourself, Is this the way I would like to be treated?

7. Create a workplace that is efficient and physically comfortable. Consider your employees' health, time and happiness when buying furnishings and equipment. Don't skimp if it will make someone's job easier. I held out for more than a year before replacing our old copier machine, but it was money well spent. Our mail room assistant is much happier now that she has a faster machine that doesn't break down. The biggest benefit is that she gets more work done each day.

8. Create an attractive workplace that gives employees a sense of pride. When I worked at a big company, I always wondered why the walls were painted gray. It costs no more to paint the walls a bright color. I resolved that when I started my own business I would make the office as bright and inviting as possible. Many of my employees have commented on the beauty of the office and how pleasant it is to come to work in the morning. Best of all, they tend to keep a beautiful office neat and organized, which is great for productivity and efficiency.

9. Encourage employees to ask questions and make suggestions. Listen to their ideas. Implement the ones that will improve productivity and sales or add to a general sense of well-being in the work environment. Check out Martin Edelston's book, *I Power* (Barricade Books, 1992) for more ideas on encouraging employees to make useful suggestions.

10. Spread the excitement. Let employees know when things are going well, and don't keep them in the dark when there are problems. There's no reason to notify them about every setback, but you might tell them, for example, that cash flow is tight and you need their help. When talking about problems, don't scare them into thinking that the end is near.

Identifying Stumbling Blocks That Can Impede Your Plans

We all bring an ample supply of emotional baggage into the business situation. Despite our best intentions, there are times when we feel frustrated, impatient, angry or just plain insecure. If this happens occasionally, there's nothing to worry about. But if you are having difficulties with your employees on a regular basis, there could be some emotional stumbling blocks standing in your way. For women entrepreneurs, these stumbling blocks often fall into three categories with specific recurring issues.

Treating Employees Like Family or Friends Is a No-Win Situation

Some women entrepreneurs tend to view their employees as family. This is fine to a certain extent, but employees are not your family, or even your friends. Don't drag personal emotions or relationships into the business situation. Beware of the following types of behavior:

- Becoming extremely angry over small mistakes

- Being unable to express your anger and shutting yourself off when an employee does something wrong

- Feeling personally insulted if an employee asks for a raise or decides to quit

- Confiding in employees too much

- Reacting as if your employees are purposely making mistakes to spite you

Seeking To Be Liked Can Be a Trap

Most women have been socialized to be liked, not necessarily to succeed. Or to put it another way, women have been socialized to succeed by being liked. If unconsciously it's more important to be liked than to succeed, how can you deal with an employee who isn't doing a good job? If you criticize the employee, he or she may not like you very much. If you fire the employee, you definitely won't be liked. If you have trouble being a good motivator or leader, perhaps your behavior is being driven by the need to be liked.

Some of the symptoms of this problem include:

- Feeling guilty or uncomfortable when you admonish an employee

- Allowing an employee to convince you that you are the one who is wrong

- Having difficulty saying no to employees when they make unreasonable requests

- Being overly concerned about whether an employee likes the job or likes working for you

- Doing or saying things to please the employee

There's nothing wrong with wanting employees to like you. The problem occurs when your behavior towards them is overpowered by this emotion.

Lack of Confidence Can Trip You Up

A third stumbling block is the lack of self-confidence in running a business. Women have not been taught to view themselves as clear-headed thinkers who can make tough decisions.

Sometimes this translates into being a wimp, and sometimes it translates into being overly tough with employees. Neither is the best way to motivate staff.

Some signs of low self-confidence include:

- Having difficulty evaluating an employee's performance

- Turning over too much responsibility to employees instead of handling it yourself

- Being afraid to give up responsibility

- Expecting an employee to solve problems that are beyond his or her grasp

- Being overly tough on or unforgiving of mistakes

You're not alone if you are suffering from low self-esteem. It's a persistent problem for women in our culture. Don't enhance the problem by berating yourself. Instead, try some of the following tips.

Overcoming the Stumbling Blocks

The first step in overcoming these stumbling blocks is to recognize that you may be responding inappropriately because of your own emotional baggage. But be careful not to blame yourself or to focus solely on the negative. Negative thinking is another emotional trap.

Next, consider the fact that the relationship between a small-business owner and an employee is not an equal one. You have control over whether or not your employees keep their jobs. This is different from the structure in large corporations, where employees generally report to bosses who cannot fire them without obtaining approval from their own bosses or others within the firm. As a small-business owner, you have the final say. This means that underneath it all your employees may be a little scared of you. Therefore, you don't have to be either a tyrant or a wimp because you already hold all the cards. You have all the power you need to be a terrific motivator and a wonderful employer. You just need to use your power wisely.

To help you gain perspective on your behavior, try to identify the situations that stand in your way in working with employees. Make a list of situations when your behavior seems inappropriate—whether it's an overreaction or an underreaction—and when you do not achieve the result you hoped for.

Note the time of day when the incidents occurred and how you felt as they started. (Were you rushed, worried, concerned about money? Did you feel hungry, tired, overstimulated by caffeine?) What did you and your employee say to each other? Is there a certain type of employee who sets you off (e.g., someone who is extremely outgoing, or perhaps the opposite, someone who is extremely self-effacing)?

You will start to see a pattern. You might discover, for example, that you often lose your temper late in the day, when you're feeling tired or hurried, and when you think an inexperienced employee has not followed directions. Once you identify the situation, you can create a strategy to deal with it.

So the next time it's 4:45 p.m. and someone has made a mistake, you will know that this could be the start of one of your ugly confrontations. Only this time you will be prepared. Your strategy might be to ask the employee to come back and speak with you in the morning, when you will be more relaxed.

Or try this. Take a deep breath. Stay calm and communicate. Ask the employee what he or she thought you wanted done. Find out if your instructions were clear enough. You may discover that the person has been so intimidated by your reactions that he or she was afraid to ask questions and therefore did not know what to do. Or you may discover that the person is not experienced enough to handle certain chores and needs more training. Or, and this is a worst case scenario, you may discover after evaluating the employee over a period of time that he or she is not right for the job. Whatever you discover, at least you will be able to make a clear-headed decision about what to do—a decision that will not be tainted by a load of irrelevant emotional baggage.

Soliciting Professional Help When the Going Gets Tough

If identifying the areas that cause problems between you and your employees is not enough to smooth things out, consider seeking professional help. Perhaps this sounds extreme, but many women business owners say that psychotherapy has been helpful in running their businesses. They have been able to resolve problems with self-esteem, problems with clients, problems with their attitude towards money or seeking new business.

Many professionals in the mental health care field have experience helping entrepreneurial women. Finding the right one is similar to hiring other professionals such as accountants and lawyers. Ask for recommendations from people whose judgment you trust, and try to find a therapist who has experience counseling women like you. It's okay to meet with several therapists before making a decision.

According to New York psychologist Susan Tross, "A good therapist should be able to withstand your protests and provoke you to go beyond the limits of your current routine or level of functioning." She suggests asking yourself the following questions when choosing a therapist:

- Can I trust this person with my most difficult thoughts?

- Will I be able to talk with this therapist about things I want to hide from everyone else?

- Does this therapist have the intellectual and personal strength to question me even when I don't want to answer, and to help me get to know myself better?

In the end, go with your gut reaction and choose the therapist with whom you feel most comfortable. A good therapist can be an invaluable tool to your success, both professionally and personally.

Motivating Your Staff Is One of the Joys of Being an Entrepreneur

There is nothing more rewarding, both financially and emotionally, than helping other people, as well as yourself, work to their fullest potential. The keys to being a good motivator are clear communication, training and appreciation. Although stumbling blocks may stand in your way, you can overcome them once you recognize their existence and make a serious effort to work them out. As the head of your own company, you have the power to be a great leader.

CHAPTER 8

Networking 101

Cultivating Contacts To Promote Your Business

W hen you're an entrepreneur, you are your company. No matter how much you may want to deny it, you and your company are intimately and intricately intertwined. You are the driving force behind your enterprise and its best representative. Therefore, you have to get out and promote your organization. Right from the start, you need to tell people who you are, what your business is about and what you have to offer. Think of Diane Von Furstenburg, Ivana Trump, Martha Stewart. These women are expert promoters whose companies have been built to fit their images and whose images have been built to fit their companies.

The easiest way to promote your company is through effective networking. Networking means meeting people and staying in touch with them to further your professional objectives. It is an essential part of being an entrepreneur, and one of the best ways to find new clients and generate sales. Networking can also help you locate suppliers, consultants and employees. It can even help you find money to finance your business. What's more, networking can be the basis for creating a support system of women entrepreneurs with whom you can share ideas, problems and solutions.

Taking the First Steps to Networking Success

How do you begin? "Every day is filled with networking opportunities," says Christine LaCerva, a psychologist who counsels women entrepreneurs. "You have to learn how to recognize them. You don't need to wait for a business meeting to promote your company." According to LaCerva, many women have trouble articulating what they do. They feel they're being too pushy if they talk about the success of their ventures. "Socialization keeps women from selling themselves as being successful," she explains.

Be Prepared

LaCerva's advice is to formulate a brief description of what you and your company do. Be ready to use it wherever you are. On a plane or a train. In a friend's home. At cocktail parties, receptions, conventions, business meetings, seminars. On vacation. In other words, use it wherever possible. Then be patient. Just because you talk about your business doesn't mean that something is going to happen immediately, especially in social situations. But all of these networking opportunities do add up. Like a good scout, the trick is to be prepared.

- Be ready to introduce yourself. Be friendly.

- Explain what you do. Be interesting and be concise.

- Find out what you can about your new contact (especially what type of work he or she does).

- Ask questions, but don't act like the Grand Inquisitor. Try to determine if your product or service would be of use to him or her. This is called "qualifying." (You'll learn more about qualifying later in this chapter.)

- Give your business card and ask for one in return. Note on the card when and where you received it, and why you might want to follow up with the person.

- Let your contact know that you will be in touch. The object of the first encounter is not to sell yourself or your company on the spot, but to create an opening for future talks.

Take Advantage of Chance Encounters

I can think of a dozen situations that turned into business bonanzas for me because I was prepared and followed the simple steps outlined above. There was the time I jumped into a taxi in Chicago just as a man pulled open the opposite door and slid in. At first we glared at each other, but we soon realized we were heading for the same destination and agreed to share the ride. As we chatted, I discovered that he owned an art gallery that might need the services of a firm like mine. I told him what I did as concisely and effectively as possible, and we exchanged business cards. I must have been fairly articulate, and the timing was probably right, because when I followed up with a letter and a telephone call, I was able to arrange a meeting that led to a contract to represent his gallery. As I said, it pays to be prepared.

Cultivate Contacts over the Long Run

Some networking contacts pay off immediately, but others take a long time to nurture. Several years ago, a young woman walked up to me at the health club and introduced herself as the publicity director of a well-known book publishing company. She explained that she had seen me at various publishing events but never thought of introducing herself until she noticed me at the gym. There was something about the shared experience of sweating it out in an aerobics class that made her feel more friendly.

I realized she was an excellent business contact and invited her to lunch shortly thereafter. She had no work for my firm at the time but thought something might turn up in the near future. Well, the near future turned into several years. So I stayed in touch and placed her on my firm's mailing list to receive our promotional materials. (See Chapter 9 for information on creating promotional materials and developing a mailing list.) I also took her to lunch every now and then to see how she was doing. Not only did I like her, but I had the feeling that someday it would pay off.

Eventually, I struck gold. One day she announced that she was taking a job in another city and had recommended my agency as her replacement. She must have said some terrific things about me and my company, because at my first meeting with her former boss I could tell that the job was mine if I could make the numbers work. After three weeks of friendly negotiations, we signed a long-term contract that has been a real boon to my firm. None of this would have happened if it weren't for a chance meeting at the health club—a meeting which led to a relationship that was nurtured over the long term.

Networking Is Not a Haphazard Process

Despite the previous examples, an effective networking program is not based solely on chance meetings. Although many networking opportunities do occur spontaneously, an effective program takes careful thought and planning. You should always be looking for networking opportunities, adding new people to your networking pipeline, eliminating others and following up. Do not sit back and wait for chance meetings to lead to business opportunities. Instead, develop a proactive plan and devote a certain amount of time to it each week. The following steps will help expand your network of business contacts:

- Join clubs and professional organizations where you will meet people with similar interests.

- Attend professional seminars, lectures and networking events that will bring you into contact with prospective clients.

- Create your own networking events during which you can cultivate clients.

- Stay in touch after you meet an appropriate business contact.

The Value of Joining Professional Organizations

In comparison to the "old boys' network," women's networking systems are in their infancy. But we are quickly catching up.

Every profession has clubs and organizations that sponsor meetings and special events to promote networking. That's where you will make your best business contacts. Civic groups, neighborhood associations, alumni associations, nonprofit arts or education organizations, even the local nature conservatory also offer networking venues where you can meet a diverse group of people, some of whom will be good business contacts.

You can't join every organization, so I suggest that you survey a few of them by attending their meetings and reviewing their membership rosters. Choose organizations in which a reasonable percentage of members can use your products or services or whose programs interest you. It's not necessary to join every appropriate club, since programs are generally open to nonmembers as well as members. Ask to be put on the mailing lists of several organizations so that you can see what type of programs they sponsor. Then choose your best options. You may wish to become a regular member of three or four organizations and attend meetings of other groups as you please.

The Importance of Women's Networking Groups

It's essential to join at least one organization devoted to women entrepreneurs, such as the National Association of Women Business Owners or the American Woman's Economic Development Corporation. (See Appendixes C and D.) Or join an organization devoted to women in your field, such as the Women's Media Group, Women In Communications or Professional Women in Construction.

If there is no professional women's group in your area, it's wise to create an informal group of your own, especially if you work alone. Several of my friends in related businesses have created an informal networking system. We call each other for advice or get together over a meal to discuss such issues as motivating employees, generating sales or finding a good accountant. Sometimes, we just like to talk and know that someone is listening. Over the years, we have helped each other in many ways.

Make a Commitment To Participate

I serve on the benefit committee of a nonprofit arts group, helping to organize its annual fundraiser. I also work on the program committee of an important professional women's organization. Although this work absorbs five or six hours of my time each month, I've made many good business contacts this way and have enjoyed myself while doing it.

Arlynn Greenbaum of Authors Unlimited found her biggest client through a recommendation made by someone she met on a volunteer committee. "When I agreed to work on the committee, I never thought it would lead to a business recommendation," she says. "I now realize how important it is to participate fully in the activities of your professional organization. It gives you visibility and helps you meet people in an effective way." It pays to pitch in.

Which brings up another point about effective networking: It works best when you're not focusing solely on your own needs. Networking is very much a give-and-take situation. You will get the most help when you help someone else. So remember to introduce people to others with common business interests or needs. Give people sales leads or information on products or services they can use. Be generous (but not foolishly so) with your ideas and leads and you will be paid back in spades.

Don't Be a Networking Wallflower

The first few times you attend the meetings of an organization, you may feel shy. Most people do. I find that if I arrive early, it's easier to meet people. Once the room is crowded, people seem to divide themselves into groups and it's difficult to get their attention. Many women, once they get over their initial shyness, have a natural ability to socialize. So put on a smile, even if it's forced at first, and start introducing yourself to the other guests. Then try to follow the steps outlined earlier in this chapter to get to know your new acquaintances.

To make a networking event more enjoyable and effective, I sometimes bring an employee or a colleague. But don't let them distract you. You must stay focused on your purpose for being there. The object is to meet new people or to talk to others you don't often see.

Angelo Valenti, a partner in Valenti, Smith & Associates, a consulting firm that advises small businesses, says, "Make networking a game. Set a goal for the event, such as the number of people you want to meet. Then give yourself a reward for reaching that goal." Valenti reminds women to bring plenty of business cards and to wear clothes with pockets. Keep the cards in your pockets so that they are easily accessible. (New cards in one pocket, yours in another.)

Create Your Own Networking Events

Art shipper Racine Berkow hosts a cocktail party every year at the annual meeting of the American Association of Museums. In this way she creates a networking event for both herself and her colleagues. Recently, when the association's meeting took place in Seattle, she went a step further and organized a day-long river rafting trip as part of her networking activities. She invited colleagues and clients from Europe and the United States to participate. "What a great day we had," she recalls. "It was a lot of fun, and it brought all of us together in a shared experience. It was the kind of event that my clients won't forget for a long time."

In Minneapolis, Phyllis Hartman, who owns a photography lab, organizes official networking events in her space every month. "I invite about 50 of my clients, friends and prospective clients to come and hear a guest speaker who's an expert on a business topic of interest to them. It might be a talk about accounting or legal issues or sales. It's been one of the most cost-efficient ways for me to keep and find new business."

Creating your own networking event has many advantages. It shows that you're interested in helping other people; it presents you and your company in a positive light; and, as the hostess, it gives you a chance to meet everyone in the room. I use almost any excuse to throw parties to which I invite my clients—from a cocktail reception in an art gallery to our annual Christmas lunch at a well-known restaurant to our yearly anniversary party. Our parties always delight our clients and create goodwill for years after.

How To Turn Networking into Sales

Giving and receiving business cards is just the beginning if you want to turn networking into sales. It's useless to go out, meet people and then do nothing about it. I've spoken with women who have drawers filled with other people's business cards, but don't know what to do with them. Don't hold on to someone's business card expecting to receive a phone call. Take action and follow up.

Qualify First

Once you organize an effective networking program, you will soon discover that you're meeting more people than you can possibly follow up with in person. You will have to decide what action to take with each new contact. Should you telephone? Send a letter? Arrange a meeting? To help you decide, you must "qualify" your contacts—divide them into various categories based on the following criteria:

- Does the contact have a need for your services or products, either now or in the future?

- Does the contact have the money to pay for it?

- Is the contact in a position to decide to spend the money with you?

- Can the contact introduce you to the person who makes purchasing decisions?

- Can the contact recommend you to others?

According to Angelo Valenti, it pays to qualify people right from the start. "Everyone wants to talk about his or her business," he says. "When you meet people, lead them with questions that will help you begin the qualifying process."

But don't push too hard or people will clam up. If you are attending a networking or business event, people probably won't mind being asked questions about their work. But if you meet someone casually, be careful. Be sensitive to the fine line between obtaining information that people wish to give you and being a nuisance or appearing desperate. I know a woman who launched a company that provided temporary workers, but she offended so many people with her pushy manner (which I believe came from desperation) that she finally had to close up shop. If you're patient, you will obtain much of your qualifying information during subsequent conversations or meetings.

Follow Up ASAP

Once you decide that someone is a good prospect (and I think instinct plays a big role in this), try to follow up as soon as possible—before either of you loses the enthusiasm the initial meeting generated. I try to follow up within 48 hours.

Use the qualifying criteria outlined above to decide how you will follow up. If you think that someone is a "hot" prospect— currently in the market for your service or product or will be in the near future—then make a telephone call. Invite him or her to lunch or arrange a meeting as soon as possible. (Chapter 10 discusses specific techniques to use in meetings with prospective clients.)

For long-range business contacts you may wish to send a letter acknowledging the introduction and saying that you will be in touch again. Include information about your company in the letter, or enclose a company brochure or other promotional piece, and add the contact to your mailing list. Eventually, in order to make a sale, you will have to call or meet with the person. Be prepared to follow up. Networking as a method of generating sales is a waste of time if you don't stay in touch with the people you meet.

Who You Know Is Important

Who you know counts in business. It's much easier to get something done, to buy something or to sell something if you know whom to turn to. Networking gives you the opportunity to get to know a wide circle of people. It's an essential activity for all entrepreneurs.

Develop a program to meet people, to present yourself to them, and to learn about them. Then stay in touch. You can do this by making your chance meetings count, by joining professional organizations and by participating in networking events. Some networking opportunities will pay off immediately, and others will take years to bloom. But if you're in business for the long run, you'll be amazed at how fruitful networking can be.

CHAPTER 9

Promotional Tools

Creating Effective Printed Materials and Putting Them To Work for You

Promotional materials can create an image, tell a company's story or help sell products and services. Although promotional materials can be as big and expensive as a book-size catalog filled with photographs of a company's products, most small businesses need less elaborate materials—business cards and stationery, simple brochures and flyers. When these materials are well planned and well designed, they can help establish your business identity and aid the sales process. Without them, you will find yourself constantly struggling to tell people who you are and what you do. It's as difficult to succeed in business without proper promotional materials as it is to catch butterflies without a net. Some people can probably do it with their bare hands, but it's much easier with the right equipment.

Your Business Card Is Your Hardest-Working Promotional Tool

Perhaps the simplest, and certainly the hardest-working, promotional tool you will ever use is your business card. Yet many entrepreneurs overlook the importance of this little piece of paper.

When you work for a corporate giant such as IBM or General Motors, the company name on your card gives you instant recognition and credibility. People assume that these big companies will stand behind their products and services. But when you're on your own, you must convince people of your ability to deliver—to do a good, even a superior, job. Your card is your first step in developing a credible business identity. Since your business card tells the world who you are and what you do, make sure that it creates an appropriate image and gives people the information they need to get in touch with you.

Cute or mysterious cards are useless. I hate receiving cards that make me wonder what the bearer actually does. A professional business card should be legible, so that people don't need a magnifying glass to read it. It should contain your name and title, the name of your company, your business address, telephone, fax number and logo, if you have one.

The card should be neat and well designed. One of the best investments you can make is to hire a graphic designer to help you create your business cards, stationery, brochures, signs and other printed materials that will work together to present a coherent image. (You'll find more information about hiring a graphic designer later in this chapter.)

Spell It Out

If the name of your company doesn't describe what business you're in, then add a few words of explanation. I received a card from a woman whose company is called Potentialities. Although this is an intriguing name, it doesn't tell me anything about what the company does. The card would be a better promotional tool if it included a few descriptive words, such as "sales and marketing," which are the services the company provides.

Another card that left me wondering came from S.O.S. Management. At first, I thought the firm specialized in crisis management. But according to Isabelle Nataf, the company's vice president, S.O.S. is a bilingual firm that provides accounting services for the American branches of European companies. S.O.S. is often called upon in times of emergency—hence the name. "Some people hate our name, others love it, but no one can ignore it," Isabelle explains. It is eye-catching, but S.O.S. Management would get more mileage from its business card if it listed its special capabilities right there in print.

Cards That Work

Racine Berkow has done a great job of creating a descriptive business card. From the name of her company, Racine Berkow Associates, you might think that she owns a consulting firm or other service business. In fact, she's probably the only woman in the United States to own a company that ships precious artwork for museums and galleries.

When I asked why she named the company after herself instead of choosing a more descriptive moniker such as "International Art Shippers," she explained that when she launched the operation, her name and reputation were her greatest assets. She had been in the shipping business for a long time and wanted to make sure her contacts knew she was starting her own company. To guarantee there is no confusion about what she does, her business card displays the phrase "International Shippers for the Art World" under the company name.

The Special Challenges of Consultants' Cards

If you're a consultant and don't have a business or company name, then it's even more important to explain what you do. "Ann Smith, Consultant" is too vague, although I did meet a woman at a small-business seminar who tried to convince me that being vague is a good sales technique. "If people don't know what I do when I hand them my card, it gives me a chance to ask what they need. Then I tell them I can do it or get it for them," she said. "I just have to find the right person to get the job done." This is a cop-out for someone who hasn't quite decided what business she is in.

Eleanor Flomenhaft, on the other hand, has one of the most effective and well-designed business cards I've ever seen. She has been working as a freelance art curator for the past three years. When she first started, she wanted to find a way to differentiate herself from other less-experienced art consultants.

Eleanor had been the executive director of the Fine Arts Museum of Long Island for more than a decade. This important credential set her apart. In a stroke of brilliance, she decided to include the credential right on her business card. "It's really made a difference for me, especially in the beginning," she recounts. "When I walk into a gallery where I'm not known, my card makes it easier to gain access to the people I want to see. In some cases, people have remembered an exhibition I organized at the museum or a catalog essay I wrote. It's instant recognition." Eleanor's card is also beautifully designed.

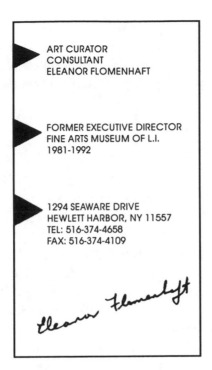

ART CURATOR
CONSULTANT
ELEANOR FLOMENHAFT

FORMER EXECUTIVE DIRECTOR
FINE ARTS MUSEUM OF L.I.
1981-1992

1294 SEAWARE DRIVE
HEWLETT HARBOR, NY 11557
TEL: 516-374-4658
FAX: 516-374-4109

Another card I like reads:

Diane Kimbell,
Freelance Secretary/Typist

You know what business Diane is in. And here's another descriptive card:

Sylvia Cole, Ph.D.
Lecturer, Therapist, Stress Management Consultant

Always Carry Your Card

No matter how descriptive your business card is, if you don't carry it with you, it won't be effective. Therefore, make sure that you and your staff carry business cards, even on weekends or on vacation. Then hand out your card at every opportune occasion. As you learned in the chapter on networking, you can never tell when you're going to meet a potential client or customer.

Stationery

Your stationery—letterhead, note cards and envelopes—should also send a clear message about what you do. Like your business card, your letterhead should be carefully designed. Basic business letterhead is 8½ by 11 inches and fits into a number ten envelope when folded in thirds. You will also need smaller note cards that fit into the same size envelope as well as mailing labels for packages. Your envelopes should include your logo and your company name and address. The rest of your stationery needs your logo, company name, address, telephone and fax numbers. You may wish to include your descriptive tag line as well.

When I started my business, I was in such a rush to tell people about it that I handwrote letters on plain stationery. Luckily, I mailed only a few before I realized what a mistake I was making. Those handwritten letters looked totally unprofessional, so I stopped sending them. I hired a graphic designer who created a logo for me that projected a sense of substance, and I used it on all of my stationery. (By the way, short, handwritten notes are fine, even cordial, but long business letters must be typed or printed from a computer.)

Choosing a Graphic Designer

Try to find a graphic designer who has created logos and stationery for other small companies. Ask to see samples of his or her work. A logo is something you will want to stick with for a long time. It's like a brand name. People will recognize it and trust it. You don't want to destroy continuity by changing your logo and stationery too often.

It's important to work with a graphic designer who can create just the right image for you. A good designer will help you choose paper stock, ink and paper color and help you determine how much stationery to order and where to get it printed. Printing is a highly competitive business, so ask your designer to get bids from several different companies. You can also get your own bids, because you are not obligated to work with your designer's printer. You'll discover that the more stationery you order at a time, the less it will cost per sheet. Base your choice of a printer on price, quality and the amount of time it will take to get the job done. Ask for samples of the printer's work before making your final decision.

Sales Brochures and Flyers

Once you have your business cards and stationery, you will need a brochure to send to prospective customers and to use as a follow-up to sales presentations. People like to be given some type of printed material to help them visualize who you are and what you can do for them.

Many entrepreneurs, even those in marketing and public relations, find it difficult to create a basic brochure for themselves. Their excuses range from no time to no ideas to no money. If lack of time or ideas is your problem, then hire a professional copywriter to help you. Follow the rules for hiring all consultants. Ask for recommendations and make sure that you see samples of the writer's work. If a tight budget is the issue, then begin with something simple. This does not mean producing a careless, unattractive promotional piece. A shoddy promotional brochure is almost as bad as none at all.

Since I had a limited budget when I started Jane Wesman Public Relations, my first brochures were printed on letterhead at the local photocopy shop. As cash flow improved, I was able to create more elaborate promotional pieces. Don't be fooled, though, into thinking that cost equals effectiveness when it comes to promotional materials. In fact, the most expensive brochures are not necessarily the most useful ones.

If your brochure costs a great deal to produce, you may be cautious about giving it away. If it looks too rich, prospective customers may assume they can't afford your product or service. Racine Berkow spent a lot of money to produce a full-color, glossy brochure for her art shipping business, but it's effectiveness has been limited. "Because our brochure looks so upscale, many art galleries think we're too expensive," she explains. "Our next brochure will have broader appeal."

Emphasize Customer Benefits in Brochures

In planning your brochure or flyer, remember that prospective customers want to know how your product or service will help them—make money, look or feel better, or get things done. If you are an accountant, this will probably mean explaining how your services will save time, energy or taxes. If you run a management consulting firm, it may mean explaining how you can help clients increase efficiency or sales.

Your basic brochure should be brief. People have a very short attention span, and too much text is daunting to read. Make sure your brochure explains:

- What your company does, sells or manufactures

- The benefits of your product or service

- Your credentials

Your brochure can also include any of the following:

- A list of important clients

- Endorsements from key customers '

- Succinct descriptions of how you've helped your clients

Keep your brochure simple in both text and design. Include photographs of you and your key employees to personalize the material. If you are a manufacturer or retailer, include product photographs. Never use overly technical terms. The brochure should be easy to read and contain just enough information to let prospective clients know how you can help them.

Apply these same principles to your other promotional materials as well. Whether it's a one-page flyer, a postcard or an announcement of a special event or sale, make sure your promotional materials emphasize customer benefits and project a coherent company image.

Developing a Mailing List

In addition to giving out your business cards or brochures at networking events, sales presentations and meetings, you should develop a mailing list and use it regularly. By staying in touch with your client base through the mail (this is also known as a direct-mail campaign), you create goodwill and sales. A well-rounded list should include current, past and prospective clients; opinion leaders; business associates; media contacts; and any other group that is appropriate for your company.

Networking is one of the most important ways to develop your list. Don't throw out the business cards you collect. Add the names to your mailing list. You can also create your list through sales calls, research and referrals. If you are a retailer, have customers sign a guest book when they stop in, or ask for their names and addresses when they make a purchase. If they hesitate, let them know that you want to alert them to special events or sales.

You can also add to your mailing list by obtaining membership rosters from organizations you belong to, or by purchasing names from mailing list companies. You can even buy subscription lists from magazines. Be careful that your list does not become too big or too generalized to be effective.

However you do it, put your list on a computer and use it. In addition to sending out your brochure, keep people informed about other things that your business is doing. Let them know that you have hired a new employee, are having a sale or have added a new service or product line. Tell them that you're going to be interviewed on television or radio, so they can tune in. Send them copies of magazine or newspaper articles that feature your company. Or do the reverse. If you see an article about someone you know, send a note expressing your admiration or congratulations. And don't forget to send Christmas and birthday cards. In other words, stay in touch with the people with whom you do business.

Keep Lists Updated and Organized

It's essential to keep your list updated—to add and remove names as necessary and to organize names by category. In that way, you can decide whether everyone should receive a particular promotional mailing or only people in certain categories. At Jane Wesman Public Relations, we keep our list of about 3,000 names organized on our computer using a simple word-processing program. Then, if we're offering a service that will interest only our book-publishing clients, we prepare a mailing just for that category.

Beyond the Mailing List: Creating a Database

If you have extremely large customer lists, you will need a software program that allows you create a database. Databases let you store specific information about each customer—for example, information about the types of purchases that each one makes. This is particularly helpful in the retail business. According to *Success* magazine, Katherine Barchetti, a Pittsburgh retailer known for her marketing expertise, has assembled a database of 28,000 customers and carefully tracks their purchases. She uses her database to notify customers about new items that will interest them or to invite them to fashion shows or sales. She even uses it to track lost customers and lure them back.

Use Your Entire List at Least Three Times a Year

Once you develop your mailing list, use it for direct-mail campaigns at least three times a year. If you can't afford to produce new promotional pieces for each mailing, then wait six months and send the same piece again. Most people won't realize they have seen it before. And if they do, it will simply reinforce your message.

Make Your Promotional Mailings Pay Off

Promotional mailings are an important way to stay in touch with your clients or customers, to generate goodwill and to develop sales. Keep your mailing list organized and updated, and create promotional materials that are well designed and well written. Even an item as small as a business card can help you project a distinctive business identity. Invest some time and energy into creating good promotional materials. Your efforts will pay off handsomely.

CHAPTER 10

Publicity

Media Coverage Can Help You Reach Potential Customers and Enhance Your Image

===============

Have you ever read an article about a woman entrepreneur and thought that your own story was just as interesting? Or turned on the radio and heard a woman business owner give advice to listeners? Or seen a story about one of your competitors in the local newspaper and wondered how it got there?

Probably none of this coverage was accidental. Someone—the business owner herself or her public relations representative—contacted the media and suggested the story or interview as part of an overall publicity strategy for her business. Publicity—obtaining stories and interviews in newspapers and magazines or on television and radio—is an effective way to promote your company. Media coverage not only helps you reach a broad audience of potential customers, but it also enhances your image and your credibility.

Don't confuse publicity with advertising. Publicity is free. Advertising is not. When you advertise, you or your advertising agency create an advertisement or commercial and then you pay a newspaper, magazine, television or radio station to run it. It will appear just as you prepared it and can be easily identified as an ad.

Publicity is more difficult to spot. It appears as an article or an interview and therefore has more credibility than an ad. With publicity, you suggest story ideas to the media and send information you would like them to use, but you do not pay them to use it, nor do you control what they say about you and your company.

In some instances, publications, particularly smaller ones, may reproduce your publicity materials directly. Larger ones, though, generally develop their own story angles. Either way, for most small businesses, publicity is more cost-effective than advertising, or can be used in conjunction with advertising to optimize results.

You Can Be Your Own Publicist

Although you can hire a public relations expert to develop a publicity program, if you are like other small-business owners, you will probably want to act as your own publicist until you have the budget to hire a specialist.

Although it takes time to publicize your own business, many women entrepreneurs are terrific at it. In fact, they often do a better job of publicizing their companies than men do. Women seem to have a knack for details, networking and follow-up, all of which is helpful in carrying out a publicity campaign.

Some women, though, are uncomfortable promoting themselves. Trash this outdated notion if you want to succeed in today's marketplace. All kinds of people—from politicians to movie stars, nonprofit organizations to governments, manufacturers to store owners—use publicity to further their cause or promote their products or services. You can use it too.

Commit to Both Long-Term and Short-Term Publicity Goals

As your own publicist, you should delineate both long-term and short-term publicity goals. A long-term goal, which could take several years to accomplish, may mean establishing yourself as an expert to whom the media turn for information about trends in your industry. A short-term goal, which could take four to six weeks to accomplish, may mean obtaining media coverage for a reception or special event you are organizing.

It's important to have both long-term and short-term goals because publicity has a cumulative effect. Over the years, as publicity about your company continues to appear, it has greater impact on clients and customers. It also becomes easier to obtain. So don't be disappointed if your first few publicity efforts don't pay off. Keep at it.

Creating a Publicity Hook

In order to obtain publicity coverage, you must decide what it is about your company that will interest the media. You need to create a story idea or publicity "hook."

For some businesses, this can be tough. If you own a printing company, you may offer better service and lower prices than your competitors, but that's not enough to interest a magazine or newspaper. If you organize a seminar, though, to acquaint people with the latest cost-saving printing and production techniques, that's probably a good angle for obtaining coverage.

Other simple ideas that might interest the media include announcements about:

- New employees or employee promotions

- New clients or accounts

- Awards you have won

- Speeches you are giving

- New services you are offering

- New products

- Successful projects

- Helpful giveaways, such as brochures, you are offering to prospective clients or the general public

Targeting the Media

Your next step is to target the media and develop a mailing list. There are three criteria here:

1. Finding the media that will be interested in your story

2. Pinpointing the media that will reach the appropriate audience for your product or service

3. Including media that might not be interested in your story at the moment but might be in the future. (It's wise to start educating the media early on about who you are. You can never tell when your company might fit into an overall article on your industry.)

The best way to develop your media list is to read the publications, listen to the radio and watch the television shows that you believe are right for your campaign. There are also reference books, such as *The Standard Periodical Directory* (Oxbridge Communications), which you can buy or find in the library, that list media outlets and their addresses. For most small businesses, the appropriate media will be local newspapers, magazines, television or radio shows as well as industry trade journals, alumni magazines or the newsletters of professional organizations.

Target Both Big and Small Outlets

Although it's a great ego boost to appear on a national television show or in a major publication such as *The Wall Street*

Journal or *Business Week*, don't expect to obtain that type of coverage unless you have a very big story to tell. Instead, start with smaller periodicals and local media that will be interested in what you're doing. Each time an article appears about your company in any size publication, you can use it to generate additional interest. Send reprints to current and prospective customers. Quote from it in brochures or advertisements. Display it in your office or store. Include it in an information package to interest other media outlets.

Although I'm not suggesting that you ignore large media outlets, there can be an advantage to small publications. They often have extremely targeted audiences, which means they reach the right people. When I began writing this book, I needed to find a company to publish it. While I was making inquiries at various publishing houses, one of my employees sent a notice about the book to a newsletter that's read by several hundred people in the publishing industry. As soon as the newsletter ran the item, I received a call from Bobbye Middendorf, an editor at Dearborn Publishing, who wanted to read my proposal. The rest, as they say, is history. Dearborn agreed to publish my book, and here it is. The point is that a publicity notice in a small, targeted publication can have excellent results.

Which leads me to television and radio. Although they can reach large audiences, the impact disappears more quickly than with the print media. There's no hard copy left once you're off the air. (Of course, you can record the segment, but it's difficult to convince people to play the tapes. It's much easier to get them to glance at a reproduction of a newspaper or magazine article.) Therefore, although television and radio coverage is important for promoting certain types of products or people, it often doesn't work as well for small businesses.

Preparing Materials for the Media

In order to capture the media's attention, you've got to send something in writing. A well-written press release is your number one tool. Additional materials include pitch letters, fact sheets, captioned photographs, company brochures or reprints of articles. If you cannot prepare a press release yourself, hire someone to write it for you. But before you do, read the following guidelines so that you know what you are paying for.

As a public relations professional, I think of press releases as mini newspaper or magazine articles, written in clear, concise journalistic style. As I mentioned, periodicals sometimes use press releases, or parts of them, verbatim. If you want this type of pick-up, then you have to create well-written material.

To prepare a press release for the business section of your local newspaper, begin by studying how the articles in the section are written. Notice that the headlines grab your attention and give you an idea of what will follow. The first paragraph of each article contains all the essential information—the who, what, where, when, why and how of the story. Additional information follows in order of importance in subsequent paragraphs. This is called the inverted pyramid style. Use it whenever you prepare a release.

To give you a better idea of how to write one, I have prepared a sample release that could be sent to industry and business publications to announce a new employee at my company (see Figure 10.1).

I have also included a sample press release that might be used by an imaginary retail shop to announce a new jewelry collection. Notice how a quote from the store's owner personalizes the release (see Figure 10.2).

Press Release Format

Print press releases on your company letterhead. Type them double-spaced, using a computer, if possible. Leave wide margins, and choose a large typeface that's easy to read. At the top of the press release put:

- The phrase "For Immediate Release," to indicate that the information can be used right away

Figure 10.1   Sample Press Release #1

For Immediate Release
Contact: L. Stuart — (212) XXX-XXXX

STEPHANIE LEHRER JOINS
JANE WESMAN PUBLIC RELATIONS
AS ACCOUNT EXECUTIVE

New York City, April 15, 19XX — Stephanie Lehrer has joined Jane
Wesman Public Relations as an account executive effective immediately. Ms. Lehrer has nearly 20 years of experience in marketing and
public relations for both the public and private sectors. She will be
responsible for working with such clients as Van Nostrand Reinhold,
Element Books and the World Monuments Fund as well as with a
wide range of individual writers and artists.

Before joining the Wesman organization, Ms. Lehrer was director of
communications for the Maternity Center Association in New York City,
where she was responsible for fundraising, public relations and the
creation of the Center's educational publications. From 1988 to 1991,
she worked at the Montefiore Medical Center in the Bronx, where she
wrote and edited employee publications and coordinated press publicity and special events. She served as a publicist with Doubleday
from 1984 to 1987, and prior to that edited Warner Cable's monthly
Movie Channel guide. She also created promotional materials for the
educational cable network, Nickelodeon, and served as assistant editor
of *Export* magazine.

Ms. Lehrer, who was raised in Manhattan, received a degree in En-
glish literature, magna cum laude, from the University of Michigan at
Ann Arbor.

# # #

Figure 10.2   Sample Press Release #2

For Immediate Release
Contact: S. Perkins — (516) XXX-XXXX

NEW JEWELRY BY ACCLAIMED SCULPTOR AND DESIGNER
VALERIE QUINN ON VIEW AT THE ARTIST'S JEWELBOX
BEGINNING NOVEMBER 18, 19XX

Just in time for the holiday season, The Artist's Jewelbox, located at 399 Baxter Street, in Port Washington's historic seaport district, will unveil a new collection of jewelry by the internationally acclaimed sculptor and designer Valerie Quinn. A reception honoring Ms. Quinn will take place on Saturday, November 18, from noon to 3:00 p.m. in the store's second floor gallery.

Using pearls, topaz and other semiprecious stones set in 14K gold and silver, Ms. Quinn has created a dazzling collection of bracelets, pins and earrings. These opulent, yet affordable pieces, ranging in price from $150 to $1,500, reflect Ms. Quinn's interest in nature and the four seasons. Each piece is fabricated by hand and is a small work of art in itself.

"We are delighted to present this new collection by Valerie Quinn," says Susan Perkins, owner of The Artist's Jewelbox. "Her work has universal appeal. I don't know anyone who isn't fascinated by the beauty and sparkle of these truly original designs."

Inspired by such natural phenomena as falling snow or waves breaking against the shore, Ms. Quinn has melded stones and precious metals into a group of sculptural forms that will be treasured for a lifetime. The pierced surfaces of her sterling silver seashell cuff highlight the wearer's wrist, while the tangled pearl ropes that compose her Mediterranean necklace are the perfect adornment for a simple black evening dress.

Ms. Quinn's designs, which have been featured in major fashion and art magazines around the world, are available on Long Island exclusively at The Artist's Jewelbox. A color catalog can be obtained by calling (516) XXX-XXXX,

# # #

- A date, if there is no date in the headline

- A contact name and telephone number to call for information

Write "more" at the bottom of the page if the release continues to the next page, and number each page after the first one. Place three number signs (# # #) at the bottom of the release to signal the end.

Check and recheck for factual, typographical and spelling errors. Wait at least a day after you write the release to send it. This will give you a chance to read it with a fresh eye so that you can make editorial changes and check for mistakes.

If you want to add a personal touch to the press release, handwrite a brief note in the upper corner, especially if you know the person to whom you're sending it. Or type a short cover note that adds information or points out something in the press release of particular importance.

Writing Effective Pitch Letters

You will need a pitch letter if you want to arrange an interview for yourself or someone who works for you. A pitch letter should be as clear and descriptive as a press release. The key to preparing an effective pitch letter is understanding what interests the media. Talk shows like to interview celebrities, politicians (both local and national), and experts who can help their audience look better, feel better, save money or make money. Publications want to interview people whose story will interest their readers.

Keeping this in mind, try to write a succinct letter that gives the media the information they need to visualize an interview with you. Include a list of suggested interview questions, presented in the order in which you think they should be asked. Some interviewers will use these questions; others may not. Leave this choice up to them. Type the letter double-spaced, using wide margins and a legible typeface.

Let's imagine that you own a company that sells and monitors burglar alarms and other security equipment. You might send the pitch in Figure 10.3 on your letterhead to producers at your local television and radio talk shows.

Illustrate Your Story with Photographs

It's helpful to send photographs with your press materials. Journalists like to see who they're going to interview or the product they're going to write about. A good photograph is a great attention-getter, but only professional-quality images are acceptable.

Most newspapers need black-and-white photographs. Magazines generally use color and prefer to reproduce from transparencies or slides rather than prints. Make sure that you label each photograph or transparency, and include a contact name and telephone number in case the photographs get separated from your written materials.

Working with the Media

Be Aware of Deadlines

Send your information as early as possible so that you have plenty of time to follow up with telephone calls. In general, monthly magazines work three to four months in advance of cover date. Therefore, in January they are working on their April or May issues. Weekly publications need material about three to four weeks in advance, while daily newspapers need material two to three weeks in advance, depending on what you are sending. Deadlines for television and radio shows vary. If they are really interested in your story, they might decide to interview you as soon as they receive your material. As you work with the media, you will become familiar with their individual deadlines.

Figure 10.3   Sample Pitch Letter

Date   (Name), president of XYZ Security Company, is
                        available for interviews the week of March 2 to dis-
                        cuss ways that ordinary citizens can protect them-
                        selves against today's rash of theft and crime.

Dear (Fill in name):
As today's headlines keep reminding us, the crime rate in our city continues
to climb. Burglaries are up 15 percent. Armed robberies have nearly doubled,
and more people than ever have been assaulted near or in their own homes.
What can ordinary citizens do to protect themselves, short of hiring their
own security force?

As president of the XYZ Security Company, I am acutely aware of these
problems, and I have some simple solutions that can help people protect
themselves, their families and their businesses from intruders and theft.

During an interview, I can discuss the following:
 1. What is causing the crime wave in our city?
 2. How can citizens work with the police to stop crime?
 3. What are the five things that burglars look for before entering a home?
 4. How can the homeowner protect his family and property from theft?
 5. What are the three secrets to thwarting a burglar?
 6. How can you stop a robbery before it begins?
 7. Are guns a deterrent to crime or a danger to the owner?
 8. What can store owners do to deter shoplifting?
 9. What should we tell our youngsters to help them protect themselves?
10. What can women and the elderly do to protect themselves if they are
    returning home alone at night?

I have enclosed information about myself and my company. As you can see,
I have written numerous articles on crime prevention and have spoken before
many civic and private organizations. I would be happy to share my expertise
with your audience, and will call shortly to see if you want to arrange an
interview.

Cordially,

(Your signature)

Develop Relationships Through Telephone Follow-Up

It's important to follow your media mailings with a reasonable amount of telephone contact. If you send information to several hundred people, that doesn't mean you should call them all. Be selective. The object is to develop a friendly, working relationship with a few key journalists who can use your information. If you develop a first-name relationship with 20 to 30 media people, then you are well on your way to obtaining excellent press coverage.

Wait a week to ten days to begin your telephone follow-up. Become familiar with the publications or shows before calling them, and plan what you will say in advance. Media people are extremely busy and are often working on deadline, so they don't have time for foolishness. I learned this the hard way nearly 25 years ago, when I wanted to speak with Helen Gurley Brown, the editor in chief of *Cosmopolitan* magazine. When she picked up the phone, I was so surprised that I couldn't get out a straight sentence. After listening to my gibberish for about sixty seconds, she said, "Young lady, when you know exactly what you'd like to say to me, please call back." Then she hung up. The next time I called, I was extremely precise.

It's useful to prepare a script before you call the press. Identify yourself immediately and then ask about the material you sent. For example, if you were the owner of The Artist's Jewelbox, you would call the fashion editor of the local newspaper and say, "Hello, this is Susan Perkins. I'm the owner of The Artist's Jewelbox and we're unveiling a new collection of jewelry by Valerie Quinn in three weeks. Did you receive our press release and photographs?" If the editor says yes, ask if he or she would like an advance look at the jewelry or would like to interview the designer. If so, make an appointment.

If the editor is not interested, try to find out why, very tactfully. Perhaps you should send additional materials such as photographs. You can also ask if there's someone else at the publication who might be interested in the story.

If the editor hasn't received your materials, give a brief synopsis and then send the release by fax or mail it immediately. The object is to get the media interested without turning them off. You want to develop long-term relationships with the press. You want to feel comfortable calling them again, and you want to encourage them to call you.

Writing Your Own Articles

Another way to obtain media coverage is to write an article yourself. Many business publications are looking for articles by experts. If you have an idea for a particular magazine, write a brief letter to the editor describing the topic and why it's significant, and ask if he or she would be interested in publishing it. Or you can submit the completed article to the editor, unsolicited, if you feel like writing it in advance. Follow up by phone, but don't be a pest. Remember that most editors are inundated with story ideas and unsolicited articles.

You can also obtain free media coverage by writing an editorial for your local newspaper or sending a letter commenting on a story that has already run. If you have a strong, interesting viewpoint, you have a good chance of seeing your material in print.

Hiring a Public Relations Agency

In writing this chapter, I've tried to give you some basic guidelines for running your own publicity campaign. But I've barely scratched the surface. For example, I haven't explained how to organize special events such as seminars, exhibitions or benefits as a means of attracting both customers and the media. There are several good books available which explain publicity and public relations in greater detail. These include *Guerrilla P.R.* by Michael Levine (HarperBusiness, 1993) and *The Publicity Kit* by Jeanette Smith (Wiley, 1991).

Your other option is to hire a public relations agency or a freelance publicist to help you implement a more complicated program. The usual rules of hiring a professional apply: Ask for recommendations from other entrepreneurs. Interview several candidates. Try to find an agency or a publicist who has experience in your field.

When interviewing prospective publicity people, ask to see samples of their work—press kits, articles they've placed or a list of television and radio placements they have made for similar clients. If you are interested in working with them, ask for a proposal that outlines what they will do on your behalf, what they hope to achieve, how long it will take and how much it will cost. Make sure that you will have approval of the press releases and other written materials and that they will send you progress reports on a regular basis. Remember that public relations people cannot guarantee specific placements, so use your best judgment to choose a reliable person or firm with whom you feel comfortable.

Whether you hire an agency or handle the publicity yourself, if you follow the advice in this chapter, you're bound to have excellent results. Developing a public relations program means committing to both short-term and long-term goals. You need to create strong publicity hooks, prepare well-written press materials and identify which media people will be interested in your story. Include big and small publications, television and radio shows on your media list, and try to build good working relationships with them. A solid public relations program will enhance your company image, add to your credibility and help you reach potential customers.

CHAPTER 11

Advertising

Combine It with Other Marketing Tools for Best Results

There are four things to know about small-business advertising:

1. It can be extremely expensive.

2. It works best when used in conjunction with other marketing tools.

3. Consistency is essential.

4. It's often difficult to measure results.

Advertising is expensive because you need to advertise often and consistently in order for it to pay off. A friend of mine who is the advertising director of a major consumer magazine insists that companies run ads at least six times a year in her publication if they expect to see results. Other experts say you should repeat an ad at least nine times to get a reaction. What's more, there's never any guarantee that an ad, or an entire advertising campaign, will work. This is particularly difficult for small-business owners because, unlike large corporations that can afford to test the impact of their advertising, most entrepreneurs are forced to rely on instinct and seat-of-the-pants decision-making when it comes to creating ads and measuring results.

That doesn't mean you should dismiss advertising altogether. When carefully planned, advertising can increase sales, enhance a company's image or promote a special event. To be effective, advertising should be used in conjunction with other marketing tools, including networking, publicity and direct mail.

Establish Goals

Before you spend a dollar on advertising, think about how it fits into your overall marketing plan and what you would like it to achieve. Ask yourself what and why you want to advertise. How much do you want to spend? Whom do you want to reach? Where will you advertise to reach them? How will you measure results? You will waste a great deal of time, effort and money if you don't establish goals before launching your advertising program.

Why Should You Advertise?

The most important reason to advertise is to increase sales. Beyond that, you can use advertising to build your business identity or enhance your image. Be careful, though, not to invest too much advertising money in an image enhancement program. Promotional materials, direct mail and publicity can be quite cost-effective in achieving this goal. Overall, when you think about advertising, you should think about selling more of your products or services.

How Much Should You Spend?

Some experts say that the ideal advertising budget is 2 percent to 5 percent of a company's annual gross income. Others say as much as 10 percent. In reality, your advertising budget will depend on the particular circumstances of your business, what else you are doing to market your services or products and how much money you feel comfortable spending. You want to set a budget that you can stick to because consistency in advertising is essential.

If you're in the service sector, your advertising budget may be minuscule, because much of your business will come from networking and word of mouth. In comparison, if you own a retail shop, you may be forced to advertise heavily because you are in a competitive market. Or you might be in an industry in which you want to advertise seasonally, at Christmas or the start of summer vacation, because that's when your customers are willing to spend.

It's useful to look at what your competitors are doing, or not doing, to get a handle on how much to allocate to advertising. It's even better if you can talk to them to find out how well their advertising programs are working. Even a casual conversation can be helpful.

Where Should You Advertise?

The right place for most small businesses to advertise is in consumer magazines, newspapers and trade publications. The key to choosing specific media is knowing who your clients are.

If you run a management consulting firm and your clients are human resources executives at big corporations, then run your ads in the trade journals they read. If you own a speaker's bureau and work mostly with meeting planners, advertise in the publications written especially for them. If you own a shop that sells home furnishings and most of your customers live within a 50-mile radius, run your ads in the home section of your local newspaper, or in the regional edition of a home decorating magazine that reaches your target market. For example, if you sell high-end, custom-made furniture, advertise in a magazine that's read by people with a high median income.

Read and Research

To pinpoint the best places to advertise, obtain copies of the publications you think your customers read. Read them carefully, and study the ads. If you don't see advertisements for services or products similar to yours, the publication may not be the right one. Conversely, if you see too many ads for similar products, think about whether you can create ads that will stand out. If your ad won't look different from the others, then choose another medium or create a better ad.

Call for a Media Kit

You can obtain detailed information about a publication by calling its advertising department and asking for a media kit and an advertising rate card. (You'll probably receive a copy of the publication as well.) Media kits contain data about the publication's circulation and its subscribers, such as their median age, income and buying habits. The rate card tells you how much the ads will cost. The smaller the publication's circulation, the lower its advertising rate will be.

Classified versus Display Advertising

Classified ads are less expensive than display ads. Classified ads are all text and are situated in their own section of a publication. They are usually organized by category. Help wanted ads and real estate listings are examples of classified ads. In comparison, display ads are interspersed throughout a publication and are generally a combination of text and graphics. Full-page fashion ads in major women's magazines are examples of display advertising. If you have a tight budget, running a consistent series of classified ads in carefully targeted publications can have a powerful impact on sales.

Consider Cable Television

Historically, television has been too expensive for most small businesses to use for advertising. Television commercials are expensive to produce, and you pay dearly for the privilege of reaching a large audience. If your product has mass appeal, like soft drinks and cars, then it's fine. But if you have a targeted customer base, television commercials are not cost-effective. During the past few years, however, local cable television has become a reasonable advertising vehicle for some small businesses, especially those that serve a particular neighborhood. If you own a business such as a dry cleaning establishment or a coffee shop, investigate advertising on local cable tv. The rates can be quite affordable.

Radio Can Also Work

Radio is less expensive than television and reaches a larger market than cable. It can be an effective outlet for retail shops that want to advertise a sale. Unlike a print ad that lasts all day if it appears in a newspaper or all month if it runs in a magazine, a radio commercial has a very short life span. Once it airs, it disappears into time and space. Therefore, make sure you run the commercial often enough to generate results.

Other Advertising Alternatives

Placing ads in the yellow pages or professional directories; running ads in the program brochures of fundraising events; participating in direct-mail coupon packs; and advertising on subways, buses or billboards can all be effective ways to spread the word about your company. Of course, some of these advertising vehicles are more expensive than others. But most small businesses can benefit from inexpensive ads in the telephone yellow pages or in professional directories. Retail establishments can do well by participating in direct-mail coupon packs, while a service provider may choose to advertise in an appropriate program brochure. If you think any of these options are right for you, analyze the costs. Some of these vehicles can be surprisingly effective.

Working with an Agency

If you feel on shaky ground when it comes to planning an advertising campaign, consider hiring an advertising agency. In addition to giving you an overview of what works in your industry, the agency can write and produce the ads, help you set a budget, and decide where and how often the ads should run.

Agency fees are based on a percentage of what you spend to advertise. But that doesn't mean the ads will cost you more. When agencies buy ad space from a magazine or newspaper, they receive a professional discount of about 15 percent. They then bill you for the full cost of the space. If you were to purchase the space directly from the publication yourself, you would not receive the discount unless you, too, were an accredited advertising agency. Therefore, it should not cost you more to run an ad through an agency. The same situation applies to television and radio, although discounts vary tremendously depending on the amount of time an agency purchases.

Advertising agencies also charge their clients for design, production and related expenses. Try to find one that works with small businesses and can stick to your budget. Request an estimate of costs, and always ask to see the agency's portfolio. Some agencies will also prepare a sample campaign for you, if you are planning to advertise heavily. Make sure the agency you hire understands your message and can help you articulate it. And remember, even advertising agencies can make mistakes. Monitor their work and their results carefully.

Writing Print Ads That Get Results

If you choose to handle your advertising yourself, you will need to create ads that get results. The best ads are uncluttered, uncomplicated and stand out in a crowd. Display ads are short on text and long on illustrations or photographs. Classified ads are coherent, informative and intriguing.

Follow these rules for creating effective ads:

- Don't try to sell everything to everyone at once. Focus on one or two ways that customers will benefit from your service or product. Do you provide greater convenience, better service, lower prices, better quality or more creativity than your competitors? Emphasize the quality that makes you stand out.

- Short, snappy headlines that grab the reader's attention are a must. Think about your favorite ads. All of them have memorable headlines.

- Good graphics or an eye-catching photograph are essential in display ads. A photograph of a beautiful couch, for example, will sell more furniture than a full page of descriptive text.

Make Ads Easy To Read

There seems to be a trend lately to create mysterious ads, or to use typefaces and logos that are impossible to decipher. That's fine if you're running a million-dollar campaign and you want to build the mystery to a stunning climax. But it's not going to work if each ad needs to result in sales.

I know a store owner who insists on running ads that feature a photograph of the facade of the historic building where she's located. She believes this has some type of snob appeal and will attract customers. Unfortunately, no one knows what she's selling, and her advertising budget is quickly disappearing. Her shop will too, if she doesn't change her strategy.

Seven Advertising Rules You Can't Afford To Break

1. Don't waste money on advertising that doesn't enhance your other marketing efforts.

2. Create ads that are consistent with your brochures, promotional pieces, stationery and signs.

3. Make sure your logo or other identifying trademark stands out in the ad.

4. Include your name, address, telephone number and ordering details in large enough type so that customers have no trouble finding you.

5. Use color, if you can afford it, to call attention to your ad and to highlight important information. Make sure the color matches your other promotional materials.

6. Limit the number of typefaces you use.

7. If you hire a graphic designer to create your advertising layouts, explain what results you want to achieve.

Monitoring Results

There's no sense in committing to an advertising campaign if you don't monitor its effectiveness. I recently asked a group of women business owners to discuss their advertising programs. They felt lukewarm about their efforts, and some even wondered why they bothered. Since none of them was monitoring results, they had no idea whether their ads were working or how they could be improved. Unfortunately, this is true of many small-business owners, not just women.

To measure the effectiveness of your advertising program:

- Keep an eye on sales and profits. Have your profits, not just your sales, grown since you started advertising? Check on a weekly, monthly and annual basis.

- Track your customer base. Always ask customers how they heard about you. This is essential, not only as a test of advertising, but as a test of your overall marketing strategy. You need to know where your customers are coming from, whether it's direct mail, publicity or word of mouth.

- Include an offer in your ads, asking prospective customers to contact you for a brochure, a discount or a free gift. Then track the response. After they obtain the free incentive, monitor what they buy and how much they spend.

- Include a mail order coupon so that customers can buy directly from you. Again, track the results.

What To Do if Your Ads Don't Work

If you aren't getting the results you envisioned from your ad campaign, don't panic. You created an advertising budget that you felt comfortable with to make sure that you didn't cancel your ads before they had a chance to be effective. If after a reasonable amount of time you find that your ads still aren't generating enough in sales, then consider the following:

- Your ads are running in the wrong medium.

- Your ads are not offering the right benefit, product or service.

- The ad itself—the look, the design, the text—is wrong.

Each of these components needs to be tested separately. If you want to test the medium, then you will have to run the same ad several times in different publications or on different television or radio stations, and track the results. If you want to check the benefit you're offering, or the ad itself, then run different ads in the same publication and track results. In reality, testing your ads can be fairly complicated and deserves a longer explanation than I provide here. In his book *Guerrilla Advertising* (Houghton Mifflin, 1994), Jay Conrad Levinson demonstrates what to do. The book also has valuable information for creating effective advertising programs. It's worth reading.

Two Money-Saving Tips

Make It a Team Effort

If you can't afford to advertise, think about teaming up with other businesses. For example, New York City has many office buildings that are filled with art galleries. Galleries at the same address often join together to run an advertisement in *The New York Times* listing each of their individual exhibitions. In this way, potential clients know exactly what's on view, and the galleries spend about a tenth of what they would normally spend for an ad in New York's most prominent newspaper.

The Advantages of Barter

Bartering is another way to save money. Many publications, radio stations, even tv stations will barter advertising space for products or services. Restaurants, for example, often exchange meals for advertising space. Even my own public relations agency was able to trade services for a series of half-page ads in a major industry trade magazine. We agreed to publicize the magazine, and in return the magazine ran our ads at no cost. We would not have been able to afford the ads otherwise. The ads brought us new business and were a real boost to our image. Many people mentioned them to us long after they appeared in the magazine.

If you do decide to barter for ad space, don't waste it. All the same principles of creating effective ads and placing them in the right media still hold.

Combine Advertising with Other Marketing Efforts

I have suggested that you combine advertising with your other marketing efforts. Let me give you an example of what I mean. My company recently organized a panel discussion for a non-profit arts organization. The organization needed to sell 500 tickets to make a healthy profit. Although the organization ran ads in the arts section of a weekly newspaper, most of the ticket sales were the result of direct mail and publicity. We researched a list of 3,000 people who we believed would be interested in the event and sent them postcard invitations, which were less expensive to produce and mail than formal invitations. We then sent flyers to other nonprofit arts organizations, to art galleries and to art schools and asked them to post them on their bulletin boards. We also sent press releases to local newspapers and magazines to obtain free listings. Finally, we got on the phone and personally invited our friends and contacts. We sold more than 500 tickets and had to turn people away at the door. Advertising alone would not have created this kind of a turnout, at least not in a cost-effective manner. We needed to combine it with other marketing strategies.

Since advertising can be an expensive proposition, it's essential to plan it carefully, integrate it into your overall marketing strategy and monitor results. If you pay attention to your advertising program, you will avoid the problems that plague so many small businesses when it comes to spreading the word about their services and products.

CHAPTER 12

Leave Your Ego at the Door

Four Steps to Successful Sales

A wise saleswoman once said to me, "The most important rule about selling is a simple one—leave your ego at the door. Don't turn selling into a contest of wills, a clash of egos or a forum for bragging," she warned. "Customers don't want to hear how great you are. They want to know how you can help them."

Don't Let Ego Overcome Sales Sense

Melissa Caldwell is an extremely talented graphic designer who spent ten years on the staff of one of the country's top design firms. By the time she decided to open her own shop, she had an excellent portfolio filled with innovative design solutions. But despite her talent, she had problems selling her services. When I asked her to describe a typical sales call, it became apparent that if a prospective client did not praise her work lavishly, she became defensive. She tried to persuade prospects that she was a great designer instead of focusing on what they needed and how she could help. Her need for ego gratification overcame her ability to sell.

It's easy to understand how Melissa felt. As an entrepreneur, you take pride in your company or work, and you want others to appreciate what you do. But if you take selling too personally, you will find yourself in many no-win situations. Since selling is the lifeblood of your business, you need to step back and view it with a dispassionate eye. For most businesses, there are four steps to successful sales.

Divide the Sales Process into Four Steps

If you're like me, once you start your business, you will immediately go out and begin selling your services or products without any formal sales training. How else can you keep your company going? After three frenzied years of pitching new business, I learned that selling can be thought of as a science, or as a game with clear-cut rules. The sales process can be divided into four progressive steps, and each step needs to be completed before going on to the next.

When you view selling as a science or as a game, it's easier to be objective in your approach. As in any competition, you realize that you can't always win, and that a loss is just another learning experience.

Step One—Prospecting

The first step in selling is prospecting for new customers. This should be done on an ongoing basis. No matter how much business you have, you need to keep your sales pipeline open so that you don't wake up one day with no new customers.

Research Your Prospects   Networking, as described in Chapter 8, is a great way to find potential clients, but cold-calling is the other accepted method. You have probably received telephone calls from strangers trying to sell you magazine subscriptions or new stock offerings. These cold-callers obtain huge lists of names from the telephone directory or other sources and just keep calling until they make a sale.

This is not the type of cold-calling I'm suggesting you do as a business owner. Instead, you should create a system to research potential customers before contacting them, so you know you are offering something they can use. For example, if you are an interior designer, you might decide to target businesses that are moving into new office space. There's a good chance they will need your services.

How will you find them? By reading newspapers, business and real estate publications and trade journals. You can obtain additional leads by visiting office buildings and finding out who recently signed a new lease. Or you can develop relationships with real estate brokers who can give you leads. Use whatever strategies work for you.

Once you have a list of prospective clients, call each one and ask who is in charge of decorating the new offices. If you feel comfortable, dive right in and make an initial presentation over the phone to the appropriate person. Or, if you prefer, send a letter or brochure first. Then follow up with a telephone call.

Plan Your Phone Presentation　If necessary, prepare a script for your phone presentation. Introduce yourself at once and explain the purpose of your call. Your tone of voice is important. Be friendly and positive. Remember that you're cold-calling, so you probably will be confronted with many rejections. Don't take it personally. Leave the door open for future business. Ask if you can call again at a later date, and go on to the next prospect. When you do reach a prospect who is interested in your services, arrange a meeting. At that point you are ready to go on to step two of the sales process.

Use Direct Mail To Develop Sales Leads　Another way to develop a targeted list for cold calls is to begin with an inexpensive direct-

mail campaign. Let's imagine that you're a photographer special-
izing in executive portraits for corporate brochures and annual
reports. You can purchase mailing lists of corporate communications directors, public relations agencies and graphic design
firms. Send them flyers with a return coupon or postcard (make
sure the presentation is professional), explaining what you do
and asking them to contact you for more information. Those
who respond can form the basis of your cold-calling list.

Step Two—Uncovering a Prospect's Needs

Many women rush this step. Before you can help prospective
customers, you must find out what they need. You will generally gather this information during a face-to-face meeting.

If you're lucky, your prospect will be able to articulate his or
her needs, but this is often not the case. Some people may need
a particular service or product, but insist on something else.
Others may have unrealistic ideas about what they can afford.
Still others may sound as if they know what they want but are
actually just guessing. Be patient, and ask questions that will
help people clarify their needs.

Listen Carefully   Eliciting information from the prospect is the
most important part of the sales process. Until I understood this
step, I often jumped ahead and made my sales pitch too early.
This is a big mistake. You cannot assume that you know what
your clients need or what is best for them. Moreover, prospective clients don't want to feel that you are pressuring them into
making premature decisions. This may mean listening to them
for an extra ten minutes or scheduling another meeting.

People have different reasons for buying, and you want to
discover what will motivate them to buy from you. One person
may buy based on price. Another may buy because of convenience. A third may want status. A fourth may be interested in a
service warranty. A fifth may want all of the above. When you
finally make your sales pitch, you want to know what is most
important to the client. Focus your presentation on those needs.

To keep the meeting on track, prepare your questions in advance. When I go to see a prospective client, I might ask: What is your objective in hiring a public relations firm? What do you expect to obtain from this publicity campaign? What results are you looking for? Modify these questions to suit your business. Listen carefully to the answers. Do not interrupt or try to present a solution before a client has told you everything. And take notes. You will probably need them to develop your sales pitch. Moreover, nothing makes a prospective client feel that you're listening as much as note taking and direct eye contact. Never appear distracted.

The Question of Money   One of the biggest problems in step two is answering a prospective client's questions about money. I generally try to avoid discussing fees until I have enough information to develop a program for the client. I don't want to end up defending my fee structure before I've had a chance to present the benefits of my services.

If you sell a product or service with a fairly standard and competitive price, this might not be a problem for you. But remember that once you state a price, you cannot raise it. This will kill the deal. Lowering the price slightly is acceptable, and may actually help you make the sale.

Step Three—The Sales Pitch or Presentation

After you discover what your prospect needs, you can begin your pitch. If you own a retail store, this may mean showing the customer a selection of appropriate items, describing their features and benefits and answering questions. Remember that during step two you worked hard to discover what would motivate your customer to buy. When you answer questions and talk about the product, try to emphasize these points.

Plan Your Presentation   If you are selling an expensive or complicated item or service, plan your sales presentation carefully. I begin my presentations by reiterating the prospect's needs and asking if I have noted all of his or her concerns. I then give an example of how we solved a similar problem in the past and how the client benefited from our work. I follow with specific recommendations for the current situation, always emphasizing the benefits of our service, not its features.

Know the Difference Between a Benefit and a Feature   Understanding the difference between benefits and features is essential in selling. People buy benefits. For example, my firm prepares monthly client reports. This is a feature of our services. The benefit is that the client is aware of what we're doing at all times. Therefore, I wouldn't tell a prospect, "We'll send you monthly reports." Instead I would emphasize the benefit by saying, "You'll never have to worry about what we're doing for you, because we'll report to you in writing every month."

If you were selling ski clothes, you might mention a parka is composed of the latest space-age fabrics. This is a feature. You would then emphasize the parka's warmth and resistance to water. That's a benefit. If you were selling exercise equipment, you might say that a treadmill is easy to use. That's a feature. If you emphasize how quickly the prospective customer will see results, that's a benefit.

Make Sure the Prospect Is Listening   Make sure the prospect is listening to your sales presentation and that he or she understands what you are talking about. I do this by asking, "Does this make sense to you?" or "Do you think this would work for you?" I wait for the reply.

Turn Objections into Selling Opportunities   The sales presentation is also the time when customers begin to raise objections. Do not become upset or defensive. Objections occur in all selling situations and usually involve the following:

- Price (too expensive)

- Product or service features (wrong ones or not enough)

- Timing (prospect is not ready to buy)

- Competition (prospect is looking at other possibilities)

- Guarantees (prospect fears that product or service will not be delivered on time or will not work)

If you have established a sense of trust with prospective customers, it will be easier to overcome their objections. Answer their questions honestly and succinctly, but do not dwell on the objections. Emphasize other benefits that are important to the prospect and try to negotiate a compromise.

Don't Undervalue Your Service or Product   As a business owner, you have certain flexibility in negotiating that a salesperson lacks. You don't have to check with your boss to give a discount or to add an extra carrot to the deal. But women are notorious for undervaluing their products and services. Don't fall into the trap of charging too little or offering too much because you're scared of losing the sale. If price is the sole objection, then the deal wasn't right in the first place.

Step Four—Closing the Deal

Many experts say this is the toughest part of selling. But if you progressed smoothly through the first three steps, by the time you reach step four, the deal will be within your grasp. It's amazing, though, how simple it is to blow it. All you have to do is not ask for the sale.

If you don't say something like, "Do we have a deal?" "Would you like to take the coat?" "May I prepare the contract?" the customer may never say yes. If the prospect has the money and authority to buy and you overcame his or her objections, there's little that can stand in your way of closing the sale, as long as you ask for it.

Yet many women feel uncomfortable—overly aggressive, unladylike, guilty—taking this final step. Some fear rejection. Others are afraid of failure. Don't let these attitudes stand in your way. You are trying to help your prospect by providing something he or she needs. You spent valuable time coming up with the best solution. Neither of you will benefit if you walk away from the sale without asking for it.

What To Do When You Can't Close   If you ask for the sale and the customer says no, stay calm. Perhaps there's a hidden objection that you didn't address during your sales presentation. Try to discover what's holding the prospect back. You may still have time to overcome the objection. If not, don't kick yourself for losing the deal. As a top sales executive said to me when I first started my business, "Don't worry about the ones that get away. There's always another client out there."

Fear of Competition May Be Standing in Your Way

If you find that selling your products or services is something you hate to do, perhaps a negative attitude towards competition is standing in your way. If so, you're not alone. Many women hate to compete, especially since our culture rewards competitiveness in men and boys, and discourages it in women and girls. When I was growing up, one of the worst things you could say about a girl was "she's too competitive." The implication was that she was self-centered and uncaring. If you were taught that competing openly is inappropriate, how can you possibly enjoy doing it?

For women business owners, this can mean that instead of feeling invigorated by a sense of competition, they hold back and don't go the extra mile to make a sale. Sometimes this is a conscious decision, and sometimes women don't even know they're doing it. They make excuses, saying they didn't really want the new account, or, worse, they sabotage their best efforts by not preparing thoroughly for a client meeting or by being late with a sales proposal.

You Must Compete To Win

If you feel uncomfortable with the notion of competition, how can you learn to enjoy it? Although you'll probably get better at competing in business just by doing it, it's amazing what you can discover about yourself and your feelings towards risk taking by participating in a sport or other pastime that is unrelated to your work but involves competition.

I enjoy tennis. The sport has taught me how to compete, how to be tough enough to win, how to be accepting, but not devastated, when I lose. It has taught me to believe in myself, to have courage and to persevere. Sometimes, when I'm stuck in a difficult selling situation, I remember a particularly arduous tennis match. I think about how focused I became during the game, how I shut out all thoughts of losing, how I concentrated on what I was doing, how I endured and finally triumphed.

Apply What You Learn in Other Competitive Situations to Your Business

Tennis has also shown me that if I'm scared or think I'm going to lose, I usually do, and by a lot. But if I maintain a positive attitude, I play better and enjoy the experience more.

The same is true in business. If you worry too much about losing an account, not making a sale or not winning in a competitive bidding situation, then you torture yourself needlessly. You also don't compete as well. If you're trying to pitch new business and are overly anxious about the outcome, your entire presentation can be disrupted by your negative thinking. Your reactions are not as sharp. You may misinterpret what's being asked of you and become defensive or rambling. Or you may not pay attention to the impact you're making on the other party. It's not surprising, on the other hand, to discover that you sell more or do your best work when you are relaxed and not worried about the outcome.

The More You Compete, the Greater Your Chances of Winning

Another thing you learn by participating in a competitive pastime is that the more often you compete, the greater chance you have of winning. This is true because of the laws of probability and because the more you play, the more experienced you become. When you translate this into business terms, it means that the more new business you try to obtain, the more you negotiate, the better you will become at it.

Remember that selling, too, is a game—a numbers game. Depending on industry you're in, you might have to pitch ten, fifteen, perhaps thirty prospects to make one sale. So banish negative thinking. Learn to view the sales process objectively, and keep your spirits up. Nothing sells like enthusiasm. It takes plenty of courage, energy and determination to succeed as an entrepreneur. And selling is the place where it counts the most.

CHAPTER 13

The Importance of Cash

Collecting Money Without Guilt, Fear or Anger

In business, cash flow is everything. You need cash to pay your rent, your employees and your suppliers. You won't be in business for long if you can't cover these expenditures. Therefore, no matter how much you sell, you're in deep trouble if you don't get paid. Although this may seem obvious, many women feel awkward trying to collect money, so they ignore the fact that it's due and focus on other parts of their business, sometimes with disastrous results.

I recently heard about a manufacturer who, after ten successful years, suddenly found herself on the verge of bankruptcy. She tried desperately to get financing, but wherever she looked she was turned down. After firing half her staff, she finally called in an expert to see if there were some way to save her company.

After three days of auditing her books, the expert found a simple solution. Collect the money that was due. Her accounts receivable were huge. Customers owed her more than enough to cover her debts and stay in business. Yet it had never crossed her mind to collect from them to pay her bills. As soon as she made a concerted effort to collect, she was able to stave off bankruptcy. What's more, she discovered that her company was solvent. From then on, she established stricter payment requirements for all customers and made sure that money was collected in a timely manner.

A business can go belly up quickly when cash flow is poor. Think about your own company. Could you last for six months without getting paid? How about three or four? If you depend on one or two big clients or sales, you can quickly get into trouble if they fail to pay on time.

I have a friend who ran a computer consulting company. Business was good for several years. Then she let one customer cause her collapse by extending him too much credit. Since the customer kept promising to pay, she continued to supply him with computer personnel, covering their fees herself. She was scared that if she stopped servicing the account, she would never see a dime. Well, she never did. Her fear of losing the client kept her from acting in a practical, businesslike manner. She lacked the courage to stand up to the client and insist on being paid. She didn't have to do this by herself, anyway; she could have hired a collection agency or asked her lawyer for help.

But she was trapped in a downward spiral. Instead of cutting her losses and moving forward to look for new business, she kept focusing on this one client, hoping to be reimbursed. In the end, he declared bankruptcy. By then, my friend had acquired so much debt that she, too, was forced to shut down. Although she was able to find work at another firm, losing her business was a devastating blow.

The Myth of Being Too Demanding

Many women worry that they will jeopardize their relationships with their clients by trying to collect payment. They sense that there is something improper—too demanding—associated with asking for money. Or else they feel subconsciously that they are not quite worthy of being paid. If they were, then they wouldn't have to ask for it. Other women are afraid they will ruffle someone's feathers. Perhaps they will. But it's a risk they must take if they wish to stay in business.

Don't let anyone, including your own subconscious, make you feel guilty about asking for money that is rightfully yours. You need to get paid on time so that you can pay your own bills. If you don't, you run the risk of bankruptcy. A prominent woman-owned advertising agency had to file for bankruptcy protection because several clients, including a foreign government, were slow in paying their bills. The agency's president was quoted as saying, "We were too nice for too long. We really didn't believe people wouldn't pay." The next time you feel uncomfortable asking for a check, think of this woman's predicament. Being nice is no solution when your business is at stake.

Nine Tips for Easier Collections

In general, customers will not get upset if you ask for payments that are past due. Their excuses may vary—they were too busy to write a check, they misplaced the invoice, or they thought it was paid already—but calling will usually get them to take action. In some instances, especially when a client has delayed payment because of his own cash flow problems, stronger action may be necessary. But remember, the sooner you contact a customer about an overdue account, the sooner you will get paid. In fact, the longer you wait, the harder it is to collect. The odds of collecting money that is 30 days overdue are much better than collecting money that is 90 or 120 days late.

The key to facilitating collections is reminding yourself that you are entitled to payment, clear and simple. There is nothing unladylike, overly demanding or unusual about this concept. Follow these step-by-step procedures:

1. Make sure that payment terms are clear and have been agreed upon in writing before the project begins or the products are shipped.

2. Ask for a deposit or retainer fee.

3. If you have any doubt about a client's ability to pay, ask for credit references including a bank and other suppliers. Or check the client's credit rating with a credit bureau or a company like Dun & Bradstreet.

4. Set credit limits for all clients.

5. Bill clients early. Always send the invoice to a specific person.

6. Monitor your accounts receivable on a daily or weekly basis. Monthly is not good enough. For good cash flow, monitor accounts payable (the amount you owe) on a regular basis.

7. Begin the collection process early.

8. Learn to ask for money without feeling guilty, angry or afraid.

9. Hire a collection agency or a lawyer, if necessary.

Specify Payment Terms Up Front

Sometimes, especially when your business is young, you may be so excited about closing a deal that you don't specify payment terms clearly enough. This is a big mistake. A client must understand and agree to your payment schedule. In the beginning, you may feel uncomfortable talking about money, but this is an essential skill that comes with practice. Proceed slowly at first. Explain your fee structure and payment terms in a calm, modulated voice. Listen to the client's response and negotiate adjustments as necessary. Try to create a win-win solution that will satisfy everyone.

Once you and your client have agreed on terms, put them in writing, in a contract, a letter or an invoice. Have your client read and sign the document, acknowledging consent.

Ask for a Deposit or Retainer Fee

I won't start any project without a deposit unless I have been doing business with a client for a long time. This policy is not difficult to implement and will save you many sleepless nights. The few times I encountered an objection, I held fast to my terms. And I'm glad I did. Several years ago, for example, a small publishing company offered to pay our fee plus a 25 percent bonus if we waited until the end of the project to be reimbursed. Luckily, I said no. The company declared bankruptcy less than a year later.

Check Credit Ratings

If you have any doubt about a customer's ability to pay, run a credit check with a credit bureau such as TRW or a company such as Dun & Bradstreet. Or ask for references such as banks or other suppliers. Make sure you call the references. You may decide that the only way to work with the customer is to ask for full payment before goods or services are delivered.

Set Credit Limits

Decide in advance how much credit you will extend to each client. The first thing to consider is how much credit as a whole your company can afford to give. Then divide it among your customers. For example, if you feel comfortable extending $15,000 worth of credit at any one time, then you might decide that a special customer, such as a big corporation you have been working with for some time, should have a higher limit than others. The corporation might have a $5,000 credit limit with you, while others would have a $1,000 or $1,500 credit limit.

In most cases, establishing credit limits is an internal way to monitor cash flow. It's not always necessary to tell customers about them because the limits are for your own use. You decide that you won't provide services or goods beyond a specific dollar amount without analyzing the risk. If my friend who owned the computer consulting firm had set credit limits, she would not have continued to provide services to a company that was not paying her.

Bill Clients Early

The easiest way to develop strong cash flow is to bill clients early. The sooner clients receive invoices, the sooner they will pay, and the sooner you will be able to pay your own bills. When I started out, I felt uncomfortable sending clients invoices early. I imagined they would be insulted or think I was greedy. Eventually, I realized I was wrong. You won't insult your customers if you invoice them early.

With big corporations, this is often a necessity. Even if a contract calls for payment on specific dates, large companies pay according to their timetables, not yours. Therefore, find out what type of payment cycle your client uses. If the company pays 30 days from invoice date, send the invoice at least 30 days in advance. It doesn't matter if your contract calls for payment on November 1. If you date the invoice October 20, you won't get paid before November 20.

If the company has a longer payment cycle than 30 days, try to make special arrangements to get paid sooner. You need to pay the landlord, the utility company, the telephone company every 30 days. Your creditors won't wait more than a month for payment, and neither should you.

Monitor Accounts Receivable Daily or Weekly

In order to collect in a timely manner, you need to be aware, on a daily or weekly basis, who owes you money and when it is due. Checking your accounts receivable once a month is not often enough and can result in a sudden cash crunch, even when you think your company is doing well.

If you're having difficulty creating a system for analyzing cash flow—for understanding how much you owe and how much your customers owe you—ask your accountant to design a simple system that allows you to grasp the overall picture in a few minutes.

Begin the Collection Process Early

Although many companies send written past-due notices, there's nothing like a telephone call to get action. I generally call when an invoice is ten days past due. For example, if I send an invoice dated October 1 to be paid on November 1, I will contact the client on November 10 if I have not received a check. By then I feel I have a valid reason to ask for payment. It's soon enough so that I avoid cash flow problems within my own company, and late enough so that the client takes me seriously.

Stay Calm When You Call To Collect

Money pushes everyone's buttons. Therefore, it's up to you to stay calm when you call to collect late payments. A composed, businesslike manner will keep the conversation on track and generate the best results. In most instances, you do not want your customer to feel that you are blaming him or her for paying late. Nor do you want to come across as desperate or angry. Before you pick up the phone, clear your head of all negative thoughts, whether they're about your client or your own worthiness to get paid, and plan your call carefully. Be direct when you ask for money, and stay on the phone until you are told when the check will be sent.

If you are dealing with a large company, it's usually more effective to call the accounts payable department directly rather than the person to whom the invoice was sent. If accounts payable has not yet received your invoice, then go back to that person and find out what happened. The invoice might have been forgotten or misplaced. Try to make special arrangements to get paid quickly, since it's already past due.

Use a Collection Agency or a Lawyer

If after a reasonable number of attempts to collect you still haven't been paid, then consider taking stronger measures, such as using a lawyer or a collection agency. Remember, though, that once you take such measures, you are, in effect, ending your working relationship with your customer. But if the customer has refused to pay, you probably wouldn't want to continue working with him or her anyway.

For small outstanding bills, usually $2,000 or less depending on the city, small claims court can be effective. You can file the forms yourself, and the court will give you an appearance date. Your customer will be notified to appear as well. Often he or she will agree to settle before going to court. If the customer has a grievance, though, he may opt for a hearing. Be prepared, and have as much written documentation as possible. You can ask your lawyer for advice, although it may not be worth the expense to have him or her appear with you.

For larger sums, consider having your lawyer take some type of action. You will have to weigh the cost of legal fees against the amount you want to collect. It can be expensive. At the very least, have your lawyer write a letter asking for payment. Customers will realize that once a lawyer is involved, it could mean going to court, which will be costly for them as well as you. Most will pay before it goes that far.

Another solution is hiring a collection agency. Agencies generally charge 25 percent to 35 percent of what they collect, but it's worth it. Agencies can collect money that you can't because they understand the psychology of getting people to pay. They are persistent, and people know they mean business. Also, a collection agency is probably better equipped than you to work out a payment program with a company that is strapped for cash.

Hopefully, you will rarely need an agency or a lawyer to help you collect money. If you recognize the importance of monitoring your cash flow, if you specify payment terms clearly, and if you overcome your hesitations or discomfort about collecting money, you'll discover that most of your customers pay on time and without problems. Remember that collecting money is simply another business responsibility, like hiring employees or providing good service. Although it may seem like a hassle at first, it definitely gets easier with experience.

CHAPTER 14

The Notebook System

The Only Thing I Ever Learned from Harvard Business School

At the start of my career in early 1970, I worked for a short time for one of the first women to graduate from Harvard Business School. (The class of 1965 was the first to include women, so she really was a pioneer.) Since the job itself was somewhat boring, my boss did her best to liven it up by passing along bits of advice she had learned in graduate school. The best tip she ever gave me was an easy method for staying organized that I still use today.

I call this method the Notebook System. It works particularly well if you have trouble setting priorities, if you misplace information or get sidetracked from what needs to be done on a specific day. The Notebook System quells anxiety because once you write something down, you don't have to worry about remembering it or finding it. It's perfect for entrepreneurial women because you don't have to separate personal chores from professional duties. If you need to arrange a doctor's appointment, pick up the dry cleaning or call your son's teacher, all of these chores get marked down along with your business responsibilities. The Notebook System can help you get out from under piles of paperwork because it eliminates stacks of notes and phone messages.

I insist that everyone who works for me try the system. The key is simplicity. In fact, it's so simple that some new employees don't take it seriously. But I usually win them over once they see that I can stay on top of their work as well as my own with little effort.

All I do is write everything down in a black and white composition book, the kind that elementary school children use. A bound notebook is essential because you can't tear out the pages. So don't try writing notes in a spiral notebook or making lists on separate pieces of paper. The purpose of the notebook is to keep everything in one place.

The notebook becomes a wonderful security blanket filled with information. You'll be able to refer back to it for all sorts of important information—names, addresses, telephone numbers, essential notes—that would have been lost if you had created daily "to do" lists on separate sheets of paper and then thrown them away when completed. You use the notebook in conjunction with your Rolodex, your desk calendar and individual project folders. Here's how it works.

1. Open the notebook and write the date on the top of the first right-hand page. Then make a numbered list of everything you need to do, whether it's personal or business, whether it needs to be done that day or the following week. Don't try to prioritize. Just write things down and number them in the order they come to you. This saves time. I've tried using complicated time management notebooks where you put certain types of information in one section and then carry over additional information to other sections. I wasted so much time trying to figure out what went where, and then where to find it, that I gave up in frustration.

2. Once you fill a page, turn to the next right-hand page. Always leave left-hand pages blank at first. You can use them to make notes during telephone conversations or meetings, or you can tape phone messages or other items to them that you wish to save.

3. You do not need to create a new page or pages for each day of the week. If you only use half a page on Monday, you can add Tuesday's notes right below. Or if you don't have any new tasks on Tuesday, then skip it. You can add Wednesday's tasks to the same page.

4. Add to the list throughout the day, as new tasks or ideas pop into your head. Neatness does not count. Just make sure your handwriting is clear enough to read. The object of the Notebook System is to get organized, not to win a prize for neatness.

5. Before you begin working, look at the list and decide which items are priorities. You will probably find three or four tasks that take precedence over the others. Circle these and then number them in the margin in the order in which they need to be done. Now you have a prioritized list that only took a few minutes to complete.

6. Do not use the notebook as a worksheet for large projects. Simply list the projects, then make a separate folder for each. For example, if a project consists of calling prospective customers, create a folder for the prospect list and related materials. Work directly from the prospect list. You can use the notebook to highlight project priorities. In other words, you may discover after you make a round of telephone calls that you need to call back two prospects the next day, while the rest can wait. List these two names and telephone numbers in your notebook.

7. When tasks are completed, cross them out with a single line, so that they are still legible in case you need to refer to them in the future.

8. Refer to your notebook throughout the day to make sure you are staying on track and to set new priorities. At the very least, look at your notebook first thing each morning, again in the afternoon and before you leave, at which time you can set priorities for the next day.

9. It is not necessary to rewrite lists at the end of each day. Instead, wait until you've completed most of the tasks on a single page or pages, then consolidate the few remaining tasks on a new page. You will probably do this every three or four days.

10. If you assign work to others, list it in your notebook so you can remember what you delegated and when to check on the job.

11. Take your notebook to meetings within your company. (I use mine to run meetings with my employees. By referring to it, I can tell them what I've been doing and ask them about their projects. I then make notes right in the notebook.)

12. Do not take your notebook off your business premises. You might lose it. If you attend a meeting off premises, take notes on a separate sheet of paper. Keep the notes in the appropriate project file, or tape them to the left-hand page of your notebook.

13. If you have something to do that's important and time sensitive, mark it on your calendar as well as in your notebook. But do this sparingly. Your calendar should be used to list meetings and appointments. Your notebook is the place to list projects and chores. Get into the habit of referring to both throughout the day.

14. When you write down names of people you must call, whether in your notebook or on your desk calendar,

include their telephone numbers. This will motivate you to make the call on time because you won't be distracted searching for their numbers.

That's it. The purpose of the Notebook System is to save time, save information, set priorities and stay organized. It's like a central control station. You need to back it up with well-organized project folders, an up-to-date Rolodex and calendar. I find it particularly helpful when I want to locate someone who is not in my Rolodex. If I can remember approximately when we spoke, I can usually find the name and number in my notebook. I keep all of my notebooks for at least two years. They don't take up much space, yet they contain lots of information.

You could probably create a similar system using a computer, but computers are not great for quick note taking. With the Notebook System, you don't have to wait for anything to warm up or spend time locating the appropriate disk or file. And with a computer, where would you tape your messages and other notes? Moreover, it's very tempting to edit and rewrite when using a computer, and that's not the point of the Notebook System. You don't need perfect grammar or language when you jot down notes.

I urge you to try the Notebook System. It frees you from having to remember dozens of details and reduces the number of things that can fall through the cracks. Once you become accustomed to it, you will find it's a real boon to productivity.

Additional Hints for Staying Organized

Although the Notebook System is central to my ability to function efficiently in business, there are several other things that my staff and I do to maximize time and limit mistakes. Everyone in my office adheres to these procedures.

1. Use telephone message books that include carbons so that you can keep copies of all messages. Store the used books for at least a year in case you need to look up a name or number.

2. Keep only one calendar. Leave it in the office and list all business, personal and social appointments on it. If you keep separate calendars for work and personal life, then you'll have to check them both each time you make a commitment. When you're out of the office and someone wants to make an appointment with you, either call the office and leave a message for yourself, or jot down a note and put it in your wallet with your petty cash receipts or the business cards you have collected. If you empty your wallet every day or so, you will find the note.

3. Whenever possible, use the telephone instead of sending memos or letters. Entire projects can be stalled because a single piece of information is missing. You can often get an immediate answer by phone that will put the project back on track.

4. Use voice mail effectively. The great thing about leaving messages on someone's voice mail is that you can be very specific about why you are calling. You don't have to go through a third party who might garble the message. Plan your message before you dial. If you want someone to take an action on your behalf, leave a message explaining what you need. If you give only your name and number, you may not be called back for days.

5. Respond to internal memos and notes by writing on them whenever possible. Don't create new documents.

6. Abolish "in boxes." Work just piles up in them, and half of it doesn't get done. Instead, make a folder for every

task that is normally part of your job so that paperwork can be dealt with immediately or put in the proper folder. If you need to take an action later, mark it in your notebook. When you are ready to work on it, you can find the document in the appropriate folder.

7. List pertinent names, addresses, telephone and fax numbers on the front of project folders. For example, if a project involves outside suppliers such as printers or caterers, list their names and numbers as well as those of the client so that you don't have to search for them each time you want to send a fax or make a telephone call. If you want to locate the supplier after the project is completed, you can find his phone number easily by going back to the project folder.

8. Read your mail every day. Discard junk mail and then decide with one reading what to do with the rest. If something calls for immediate action such as a telephone call, take it. If a letter needs to be routed to an employee or placed in a folder, do it. If a letter calls for later action, file it and make a note in your notebook. If an invitation interests you, mark your calendar and make a note to R.S.V.P. later. The object is to process the mail as soon as possible without overlooking important information or documents.

9. Give yourself as large a work surface as possible. Don't clutter the top of your desk with personal objects, photographs, folders or piles of paper that you're not using. Keep all work folders in desk drawers designed for files or in holders on top of a cabinet or table within reach of your desk. Trying to work amidst clutter is anxiety provoking. It's difficult to concentrate and easy to misplace essential papers when your desk looks like the remains of a paper mill explosion. If your desk becomes a mess during the day, take a five-minute break and put every-

thing back where it belongs. The breather will give you a chance to think and to reestablish your priorities.

10. Adapt the Notebook System or any of the other tips presented here to your own circumstances. You probably have special ways in which you like to work. Instead of discarding these tips because they don't fit your prerequisites, modify them to accommodate your own work style. You'll be glad you did.

As a woman business owner, you are probably juggling a dozen responsibilities at any one time. Finding a way to organize them is essential to your success. If you need more advice than I have offered here, read Dianna Booher's *Clean Up Your Act!* (Warner Books, 1992). She offers 101 tips for organizing your paperwork. Although her book is aimed at employees of large companies, many of her ideas can be reinterpreted for the entrepreneurial woman.

And finally, remember that there are two keys to being organized: eliminating as much clutter from your life as possible and being able to easily store and retrieve everything that remains. The Notebook System helps you do this with ease. Whether or not my early boss created this system on her own or learned it at Harvard, I thank her for sharing it with me. It has been a real lifesaver.

CHAPTER 15

Workaholism Doesn't Work

Fifteen years ago, a woman started her own business and worked at it seven days a week. Whenever she took a day off, she felt guilty about not being in the office drumming up new business. She was convinced that she was missing important opportunities. After several years, she allowed herself a few short vacations, but she still tended to work at least 60 hours a week. On weekends, she played tennis for an hour or two and then went straight to the office. Whenever someone asked her to stay for lunch at the tennis club, she insisted that she had to work. In fact, she declined most social invitations unless there was a networking value attached to them. Friends tried to tell her that she was hiding in her work, but she ignored them, thinking they just didn't understand.

One summer, she finally had enough with work, so she rented a home at the beach. The house was expensive, so she spent every weekend there. Naturally, she always took her laptop computer and plenty of work with her. As the summer progressed, a strange thing happened. She began to enjoy herself. Soon she noticed that she wasn't doing much work on the weekends. Instead, she was playing tennis, going to the beach and visiting friends. She was having a good time.

She became even more daring and started taking off Friday afternoons as well as Saturdays and Sundays. What amazed her was that at the end of the summer, even though she had spent two months taking long weekends away from work, her business was thriving. She finally recognized that she had been a workaholic and that whenever she didn't know what to do with herself or whenever she felt lonely or unhappy, she buried herself in business.

That woman was me. And I can testify that workaholism doesn't work. It doesn't improve business. It doesn't make you happier or more successful. If carried to extremes, it can have dire emotional and physical consequences—high blood pressure, ulcers, insomnia and depression.

Workaholics Never Feel Satisfied

Workaholism isolates you from family and friends and keeps you from finding joy and fulfillment in life. A woman with a healthy attitude towards work may spend long hours in the office on occasion, but when she completes a project, she feels a sense of accomplishment. A workaholic, on the other hand, never feels that she has accomplished enough. She busies herself with endless tasks.

Barbara O'Brien, who runs a small printing company, told me that for years everything she did was colored by her work. It was the only thing she ever thought about. Although she appeared happy and successful on the outside, inside she was torn apart by stress and anxiety. How she felt about herself was directly connected to how well her business was doing. She had no other identity. If you asked, "How are you?" she would spout her latest sales figures. She never said she was feeling good or bad, happy or sad, because she didn't know how she felt. Things became so bad that she could barely sleep at night. Eventually, she began forgetting appointments and making other mistakes. She was short-tempered with employees and clients, and business began to drop off. The harder she worked, the worse things became.

Eventually, she sought psychological counseling. "I was amazed when I started seeing a therapist to discover that so much of what I thought was important and real about work was just a myth that I had created for myself. Unless I was a success at business, I thought I was worthless. Since I never felt successful no matter what I did, I was constantly trying to do more. I was on an endless treadmill that was destroying me." Barbara is not alone in her suffering. Workaholism is widespread in this country, and women entrepreneurs are prime candidates for this affliction.

Workaholism—The Woman Entrepreneur's Addiction of Choice

What are the special circumstances that make women susceptible to workaholism? According to Diane Fassel, author of *Working Ourselves to Death and the Rewards of Recovery* (HarperPaperbacks, 1990), it's a question of self-esteem. "Workaholism worms its way right into that place in (women) where we feel we aren't good enough. Today, the societal demands on women to be competent in multiple areas are coupled with nagging self-esteem issues arising out of the need for women to prove they are worthwhile."

If you combine the issue of women's low self-esteem with the fact that society says it is normal for entrepreneurs to work endless hours, it's easy to see how workaholism can become the woman entrepreneur's addiction of choice. It can take years for the woman entrepreneur or her family and friends to recognize that she is destructively hooked on work.

Society Promotes Workaholism

Society—and the media—promote the image of the workaholic woman entrepreneur as a positive one. For example, I recently read an article about a business owner who was being touted as a role model, in part because she worked each day from eight in the morning until eleven at night, and on the weekends spent her time reading one hundred publications to stay on top of her field. This was supposed to be an achievement, something to be admired. I doubt that anyone stood back and said,"Hey, wait a minute, this woman is obsessed with work, but she is meant to exemplify the ideal entrepreneur. Is it really true that the only way to get ahead is to work yourself to extremes?"

The media is filled with an endless supply of images like this. In a special report on women entrepreneurs, *Business Week* included an anecdote about someone who left her corporate job because she was working 14-hour days and weekends and she wanted to have a life. Since starting her own company, she works even longer and often has trouble sleeping. But, the article explains, she is happier now because she is in control. Is she really happier? Or has she simply found another outlet for her addiction to work? Again, it's interesting to see how the media portrays workaholism as the only way to succeed as an entrepreneur.

The idea that working too much is good for you pervades our society. I have spoken with dozens of women who assume that they have to work incredible hours each week or their businesses will fall apart. Although they complain about the long hours, they never take a moment to reflect on whether all this work is helpful or harmful to them. They speak as if they have no alternative.

Watch Out for These Symptoms

How can you tell if you're suffering from an addiction to work or just working hard? It's difficult, because running your own business does take lots of time, energy and hard work. Moreover, one of the characteristics of being addicted is denying that you are. It's a catch-22. If you're concerned, answering the following questions will give you a better idea of where you stand in relation to work:

- Do you often feel as if something important is hanging over you?

- Are you constantly rushing to catch up?

- Do you feel uneasy after completing an important task instead of having a sense of accomplishment?

- Do you find it impossible to delegate work? If you do delegate, are you often dissatisfied with the results?

- Do you feel that no matter what you do, something will go wrong, so you do more to compensate?

- Do you often feel tired, yet you can't stop to rest?

- Do you fear that your life would be meaningless without work?

- Do you constantly check your answering machine?

- Do you always take a cellular phone wherever you go?

- Are you constantly late, because you can't get away from your work?

- Do you cancel engagements because you need to work?

- Do you tell your family or friends to bear with you, you'll have time for them soon—only that day never arrives?

- Do you hide your work? For example, do you take it with you on vacation and do it when no one is looking?

- Do you have trouble sleeping at night, because business is always on your mind?

- Do you have any physical problems associated with workaholism such as high blood pressure or ulcers?

- Do you find it difficult to say no when you're asked to do something extra?

If you answered yes to even a few of these questions, you would probably like to find some way to slow down, but you are worried about how it will affect your business. I can say from my own experience that by gradually adding leisure time to my weekly schedule, I was able to break my obsession with work. If I had tried to do it all at once—cutting out all work on weekends and at night—I'm sure I would have failed.

Overcoming Workaholism

First, admit to yourself that you are spending too much time working and that it is having a negative affect on your life. Then decide what you would do if you had more free time each week. Would you spend it with your family? Would you use it to relax? Would you learn a new sport? Visit friends? Go to the theater?

The object is to decide what you want to do outside of work and recognize that fun and relaxation are just as important as work. If necessary, remind yourself that taking time off will help you think better and work better. It will not only add to your sense of fulfillment, but it will help you succeed.

Demystify Your Work Schedule

The next step is to analyze your work schedule. The object is to demystify your work week. By enumerating what needs to be done, you may discover that certain tasks don't require as much time and energy as you imagined. Begin by writing out a schedule for yourself for the next four weeks. If that seems daunting, then prepare a schedule for just one week. What do you need to accomplish? How long will each task take? If you have large projects to complete, break them down into individual steps. Make the schedule realistic. Allocate enough time to get each task done, but not too much time. Include meetings, appointments and other obligations.

Then examine your schedule and decide what can be eliminated. For example, you may be spending a great deal of time doing volunteer or pro bono work, telling yourself that it will lead to additional business. Sometimes it does, but it's more likely that you overextended yourself because you can't say no. Now is the time to make some cuts. If you do volunteer work for three or four organizations, try cutting back to one. If you are handling several volunteer projects for one organization, eliminate as many as you can. If you feel uncomfortable doing this, make the cuts progressively. I'm not saying that you should eliminate all pro bono work, because it's important to do something for others and to give back to the community. But overloading yourself with volunteer work is not good for your business or your health.

Eliminate Extraneous Tasks

If you find that your week is filled with other extraneous tasks, such as appointments with people who are not essential to your business, then eliminate these, too. Try to make each of your meetings as brief as possible. Be prepared with an agenda and stick to it. The easiest way to move forward in a meeting is to listen as much as possible, and then make comments that lead the other participants to the next issue.

Delegate

The next step is to delegate. Stop imagining that only you can get the job done. Hire outside consultants whenever possible, or allow your own staff to do more work for you. Be clear about what results you expect. Break projects into steps, and then allow employees to do it their own way. Check on their work periodically, whether it's daily or weekly, to make sure things are going smoothly. But under no circumstances should you take the job back and do it yourself.

Schedule Free Time for Yourself

Once you cut back on your work obligations, you can schedule free time for yourself. There are a couple of ground rules to remember:

- Don't try to schedule too much free time at first. You can add more later.

- Schedule activities that have nothing to do with work.

- Don't allow business interruptions. In other words, do not bring your cellular phone. Do not check your answering machine. Don't tell your colleagues where they can reach you.

At first, you may feel frightened giving yourself time off. That's why it's important to start by making a small commitment. For example, you might decide that you will no longer work on Friday evenings or Saturday afternoons. Don't just say you're going to stop working. Make plans to do something else, preferably with other people. You have many options for leisure activities, whether it's joining a weekly reading group, visiting a museum, having a massage or taking a class in something that is not connected to your business. If you have children, make a commitment to share an activity with them. If you are on your own, make dinner or movie plans with a friend. Make your commitment in advance, and don't break it.

Once you experience time away from work, you will probably discover, as I did, that you feel calmer at work. I found that I became more focused. I wasted less time and accomplished more because I had things to look forward to outside of work. Of course, there are still times when I'm stuck in the office on evenings, or weeks when I seem to work a hundred hours. But it doesn't happen every week as it did in the past.

Balance Is the Key

The key to overcoming workaholism is to find balance in your life. You need time for family and friends, work and leisure if you want to feel fulfilled. The first step to creating balance is to admit that you have a problem with overwork. The next step is to examine your work week and eliminate extraneous tasks. The third step is to schedule free time for yourself. And the fourth step is to gradually add more free time as you learn to enjoy it. A life composed only of business success is, in the end, an empty and frustrating one. A balanced life is worth striving for.

CHAPTER 16

18 Sharkproof Strategies for Entrepreneurial Success

1. Keep a Private Journal

Maintain a private journal about your work, your employees, your clients or customers. Include your fears, apprehensions, achievements. I began keeping a journal about five years ago. In it, I describe the problems I'm having in the office as well as our accomplishments. This information has been extremely helpful to me. For example, if I'm having difficulty with an employee, I can look back in my journal and discover that I had a similar problem a year or so earlier. This makes it easier to put the problem into perspective and to formulate a solution. Without the journal, I would not have remembered what happened or what I did to solve the problem.

A journal is also great when you are having doubts about cash flow or finding new business. It's one thing to have computer printouts and other statistics to chart the ups and downs of your company. It's quite another to have a journal that reminds you how you felt and what you did during the good and the bad times. How did you feel the last time you wanted to expand your business? What did you do to generate growth? What risks did you take? How did you cope when you lost a major client? What action did you take? What worked best for you in finding new business?

Let Your Journal Guide You

No one knows your business like you do. Yet it's easy to forget some of the lessons you learn through experience. The journal will help you remember. In my office, the period between December 15 and January 15 is generally slow, so I often feel uncomfortable at the end of each year as the number of projects dwindles. It's reassuring to pick up my journal and see that this slow period is a seasonal trend and to read about what we did to generate new sales—to learn what worked and what didn't.

Never share your journal with anyone. It is completely confidential, which means that you can write anything you want. This is essential. Your journal is your way of talking to and teaching yourself. And since no one else will see it, you don't have to worry about spelling, grammar or neatness.

2. Surround Yourself with Positive People

Negative people are a drain on your time and your energy. They will undermine your ambitions and make you question your ability to succeed. Beware, negativity comes in many forms —from people who complain incessantly about their jobs, to those who are forever belittling others, to those who are constantly strapped for money or time.

Negativity Is Contagious

Negative thinkers are unhappy people who view life as a half-empty glass. What is really dangerous about negativity is that it's contagious. Think about how disheartened you feel after dining with a colleague who spends the entire time complaining about the health of his or her business. A really negative person can make you believe that the entire economy is collapsing, just because he or she is not doing well. By the time the meal is over, you start to think that your own business is in trouble as well.

Of course, you can't expect people to be happy at all times. When something does go wrong, it's important to be available to help people out. I'm simply suggesting that when you have a choice—for example, when hiring employees, when choosing consultants or suppliers, when making new friends—avoid people who are filled with gloom.

Positive People Make Things Happen

Look for people who are optimistic and upbeat. Not only will their energy make you feel better and vice versa, but positive people make things happen. When I started my business, I used to stop by the studio of the world-famous artist Leroy Neiman. His outlook was always so upbeat that no matter what problems I brought with me, they disappeared as soon as I walked through the door.

Leroy not only believed in himself, but he believed in my ability to succeed as well. He made it sound as if success were easily within my grasp. And he did something concrete to assist me. By introducing me to the marketing vice president of one of the country's major banks, he helped me land my first big account. Without his referral, I would not have made it past the receptionist. A negative person would never have helped me the way that he did. Negative people resent the success of others. Positive people will help you get ahead.

3. Don't Be a Chicken in the Face of Customer Dissatisfaction

Don't be a chicken. When a client or customer is dissatisfied, hang in there. Don't drop the client because you are afraid of criticism or a confrontation. That's the easiest thing to do. It's much more difficult (and more rewarding in the long run) to listen to a client's complaint without getting angry or upset. After you have a chance to think about it, you can decide what to do.

Being able to listen to a dissatisfied customer takes practice. The first year my friend Melinda Jeffries ran her consulting firm, she dropped three clients who she believed did not appreciate her efforts. Once she realized that this was bad for business, she forced herself to listen to clients more carefully. She found that what had at first sounded like criticism was often a request for more information or for a more thorough explanation of what she was doing. As she learned to communicate better, her business grew and she received fewer complaints. By learning to listen, she was able to help clients before a problem arose.

Negotiate a Solution

The other response to criticism—agreeing to do whatever the client wants—is not a wise business practice either. If you constantly give in to customer demands, you do so at your own expense. Instead, learn to negotiate a solution. Sometimes, doing just a little extra will solve the problem without turning your life into a workaholic nightmare. Learn to say no politely and assertively, and your clients will become easier to deal with.

4. Project an Image of Success

You only have one chance to make a first impression, so make it count. Although your manner, your voice, your ability to communicate are essential, the way you look counts the most when someone first meets you. I know many women who hate this concept. They say that clothing doesn't make the man or the woman, and they are right. But people are visual creatures, and they can't help but notice your appearance, especially when you first meet.

First Impressions Are Based on Appearance

According to an article in *The New York Times*, "The impression people make on one another is based 60 percent on their appearance, 33 percent on the way in which they speak and 7 percent on what they say." If your clothing is sloppy, if you look ungroomed, prospective clients may not want you to represent them, nor will they want to buy from you. Their basic reaction might be something like this: "If this person doesn't have the ability to care for herself, how can she possibly take care of business and provide me with the service or product I need?"

This doesn't mean that you have to be a raving beauty or invest in expensive designer clothing to succeed. It does mean that you should dress neatly and appropriately for business— nothing skin-tight or low-cut, no dangling jewelry, no dirty blue jeans or torn stockings, no wild or stringy hair.

Let Your Appearance Instill Confidence

Keep it low-key and dignified. You want your appearance to instill confidence. I recently gave a talk before a group of women who were just starting their own businesses. I was shocked by the way some of them dressed—in old jeans and dingy shirts and sweaters. The impression they gave was not one of competence and success, but rather of rebelliousness and insecurity. I wondered whether they dressed more professionally during the business day. If not, they probably had to work extra hard to overcome negative first impressions.

Knowing that you are well groomed will boost your self-confidence, whether you are delivering a sales pitch or trying to motivate your staff. How you feel about yourself shows through in these situations.

Workplace Image Also Counts

Image and appearance also count in the work environment. When clients come to your office, they don't want to see piles of papers spilling onto the floor or a stack of used coffee cups on the edge of your desk. Everyone knows it's impossible to be organized in a messy office. Why should people trust you with their accounts if it looks like you're going to lose their paperwork under a stack of unopened mail? Don't overlook the importance of appearance, whether it's you or your office. If 60 percent of a first impression is based on how you look, why not make the most of it?

5. Don't Mix Business and Romance

Business and romance are an explosive mix that will blow up in your face. As one of my colleagues puts it, "Unless you know you're going to marry the guy, don't even think about getting involved." These guidelines apply to employees, consultants and customers alike. "Find someone outside your business. Business relationships have their own set of problems. Romantic relationships have plenty of their own. Why mix the two?" she asks.

When Rita Hamilton lost her job in advertising, she decided to try her hand as a freelance copywriter. Jobs were few and far between, but she finally started getting steady assignments from the ad department of a major retailer. Perhaps because of her vulnerability, she also became involved with the man who headed the department.

The relationship seemed like the perfect solution to her loneliness and her fears about not being able to make it on her own.

However, things did not work out. The romance was rocky from the start, and it ended in recriminations. As soon as it was over, so were all of her assignments. To make matters worse, her ex-client/boyfriend refused to give her recommendations when she looked for business elsewhere. She finally had to scratch his name from her client list in order to move ahead with her career.

Another woman business owner who runs a successful employment agency also became romantically involved with a key client. Things were going well until he asked her to supply personnel to his firm without charging a fee. She considered his request carefully and decided that it would damage her business. As soon as she turned him down, he lost interest in their relationship, both personally and professionally. He cut her off completely.

I've also heard about women getting involved with their employees and losing all perspective on their performance, giving undeserved promotions and raises. Becoming romantically linked with outside advisers can be problematic as well. In her book *Woman to Woman* (Prentice Hall, 1993), Geraldine Larkin warns about women getting involved in abusive relationships with their accountants, lawyers or bankers. She even includes a checklist of symptoms of an abusive relationship. Business is difficult enough without adding the emotional charge of romance and the problems that can arise when a relationship sours. Keep the two separate.

6. Always Return Telephone Calls

Some people think it is a sign of power not to return telephone calls. I think it is foolish and discourteous. It's also a sign of disorganization. In the end, you will save more time and energy by talking to people who want to speak with you than by avoiding them. I have often returned a call to someone I didn't know, only to discover that he or she was interested in hiring my firm, or was offering a service I needed. Of course, there are people to whom I would prefer not to speak, but I try to end those calls quickly while still remaining polite.

Another reason for returning calls is that it enhances your image. It shows that you are considerate of others and interested in doing business. People will say good things about you. It is also an easy way to network without having to go out. Not returning calls makes you seem like a difficult person, someone to be avoided. No one wants to do business with a person who is impossible to reach. So return your calls. If you are really overwhelmed, have someone on your staff return the less urgent ones. You can follow up later.

7. Ask for Advice Whenever You Can

In general, people ask for business advice only when they are in their work environment or embroiled in a problem. I try to seek advice whenever the opportunity arises, especially while traveling or on vacation. Most people are less guarded and more relaxed when they are away from their jobs.

I have picked up many useful hints from seatmates on airplanes or while having dinner at an isolated ski lodge. I have received advice on negotiating contracts, evaluating employees and finding office space. It's not necessary to demand information; just have a pleasant conversation. If your companion seems to have an interesting approach to something that affects you, ask about it. And don't forget to share your ideas. This is a give-and-take situation.

8. Don't Take Things Personally

It's easy to turn a business rejection into a personal affront and lose a week's sleep over it. The best way to overcome it is to put yourself in the other person's shoes. If you worked especially hard to make a sale that went to one of your competitors, remind yourself that only one company could get the job, and that the client probably had a difficult time making a final decision. Remind yourself of the positive things that were said to you when you got the bad news. If the client said he or she liked your proposal or thought you were extremely qualified, accept the compliment. Go on with your work. The client made a business decision in choosing your competitor. It was nothing personal.

9. Keep Overhead Low

Keep your fixed overhead as low as possible without sacrificing opportunities for growth. Fixed overhead includes things that are essential to your business, such as office or retail space, salaries, furnishings and equipment. Retailers seem most prone to fall into the trap of high overhead. During the early 1980s, I knew several women who ran successful art galleries in Manhattan's trendy East Village. The art market was at its peak. Their galleries were small, their overheads were low, and they were doing well. They all came to the same conclusion—if they moved to larger spaces in one of Manhattan's more upscale art districts, they would make more money. Unfortunately, it didn't work. Once they committed themselves to more expensive quarters, they had to charge higher prices and sell more art to make a profit. Many of them couldn't make the extra sales and had to close down after experiencing large losses. Therefore, if you're going to increase your overhead, make sure you have a plan for increasing your sales as well.

10. Look at the Big Picture

My dad gave me a simple piece of advice many years ago, when I had problems with employees, overhead and finding new business. He pointed out that I was being shortsighted. When I stepped back and looked at the bigger picture, I felt a sense of relief. Instead of focusing on what would happen in the next month or two, I looked at where I wanted to be two years down the road. I also looked back and saw how far I had come. Suddenly, the pressure was off. I had plenty of time to accomplish my goals.

11. Learn To Live with Uncertainty

Uncertainty drives some people crazy. They can't live with loose ends or unanswered questions. When they ask, they want immediate answers. When they need to do something, they worry about all the possible ramifications and permutations of their actions. Everything must be organized, categorized and settled.

Life isn't like that. It's filled with uncertainties. No one knows for sure what will happen tomorrow or next year. The more comfortable you are dealing with uncertainty, the more successful you can be as an entrepreneur. It will enable you to take risks and to leave things hanging. It will allow you to be patient and self-confident. When you learn to live with uncertainty, you will realize that some things may work out and others won't. Uncertainty won't keep you from trying.

12. Never Get Angry with a Client

I learned this lesson the hard way. If you get angry with a customer, he or she will go elsewhere, no matter how great your product is or how good you are at what you do. In your personal life, you can get angry with family and friends, and they will stick around and forgive you, sometimes instantly. Clients won't. I have never found an effective way to mend a blowup with a client. You can apologize. You can send gifts. You can beg for mercy. But I guarantee, the minute your contract is up, they will hire someone else. So beware. No matter how angry a customer makes you, keep your mouth shut. Even a biting or sarcastic response can signal the end of the deal.

13. Don't Be Jealous of a Competitor with Lots of Start-Up Capital

When I started my business, I had to compete against a woman whose new public relations agency was funded by a Fortune 100 company. They gave her a contract worth several hundred thousand dollars, and she opened her doors. I was jealous of her and intimidated by her. She organized huge, extravagant press events. She had a beautiful office in an exclusive building. She had fifteen employees compared to my one. She had it made.

After three years, she was out of business. Her big client hired another firm. Because everything had been handed to her in the beginning, she never learned how to find new business, how to manage cash flow, how to run her office efficiently.

The struggles you face during your first few years in business will become the foundation for future growth. Necessity is the best teacher of all. So don't be jealous of those who seem to have it made. No one achieves lasting success without hard work.

14. Recognize That Problems Don't Always Have Clear-Cut Solutions

One of the biggest stumbling blocks among women entrepreneurs is a sort of paralysis that occurs when they can't make a decision. They don't feel comfortable with the fact that many problems have no clear-cut answers, and that they are going to have to weigh the options and choose the solution that seems best, even if it's not perfect. Life is filled with many gray areas, and the life of an entrepreneur has more than the average share. Learn to accept that fact and decisions will be easier to make.

15. Appreciate the Importance of Time and Experience

Some things are impossible to learn without experiencing them. And you can't experience them unless you have been around for a while. You can't squeeze ten years of experience into five, so relax. More knowledge, more sales, more money and more success will come with time.

For example, I have been organizing publicity campaigns for nearly 25 years. I have employees with 5, 10, 15 years of experience. They know how to organize publicity campaigns, too. But they don't know as much as I do about what can happen—what can go right and what can go wrong. I'm aware of additional contingencies just because I've been around longer. Time is a great teacher. Appreciate its value.

16. Don't Hold Grudges

Grudges are counterproductive. Many people—men and women—believe that if they hold a grudge they will eventually have a chance to get even. But ask yourself, have you ever been able to do something equally hurtful to the person who offended you as he or she did to you? And if you did, what benefit did you derive from your action? I was at a dinner party where a woman started talking about a former colleague. She held such a grudge against him that she spent half an hour describing all of his worst qualities. Perhaps she felt that she was getting even by making a fool of someone who had once insulted her. Instead, she made a fool of herself. She appeared so vindictive that she was never invited to dinner again. The worst part was that several of the people at the party would have been excellent business contacts for her.

Another problem with grudges is that they're often based on misunderstandings or misinterpretations of what someone meant to say or do. People who hold grudges are often overreacting to a perceived slight. Many years ago, one of my employees left to take a job at a major museum. I was devastated. She gave me two days' notice and quit during our busiest season. I felt that she didn't appreciate all I had done for her. I fumed for several months. Finally, I relented and called to see how she was doing. She was delighted to hear from me. About a week later, she recommended my firm so highly that we obtained a major client with little effort.

Nursing a grudge prevents you from orchestrating a real solution to your problem. If you believe that someone has insulted you or damaged you in an important way, call him or her on it. Explain how you feel and seek an apology. That's a more effective solution than fuming. Grudges limit your ability to forge ahead. They make you shortsighted and close off opportunities. Try to eliminate them from your life.

17. Learn To Negotiate Without Letting the Inner Child Peek Through

Don't worry about being liked when you negotiate—whether it's with a client, a consultant or one of your employees. This doesn't mean that you can be obnoxious during a negotiation. That won't get you anywhere. But if you feel uncomfortable, if you sense yourself losing ground, perhaps you have lost sight of the desired outcome. You may be saying things to try to win approval, instead of furthering the negotiation or closing the deal. Don't let that inner child peek through. You don't need to be loved by your business associates. You need their respect and their cooperation. You want them to believe in your competence and your ability to make good on your promises.

18. Be Gentle with Yourself

If you make a mistake, don't drive yourself crazy with recriminations. Acknowledge that something went wrong and go on to the next project. Instead of focusing on what you should have done, acknowledge your talents and your accomplishments. Think about what makes you special and what brings joy into your life. Stand back and pretend that you are someone else who loves you very much. How would that person describe your best qualities? Now take a deep breath and be happy that you are who you are. With your courage, your energy and your determination, you can fulfill your greatest ambitions. Just dive right in—the sharks won't bite.

Business Books for Further Reading

Albert, Susan Wittig, *Work of Her Own: How Women Create Success and Fulfillment Off the Traditional Career Track*. New York: G.P. Putnam's Sons, 1992.

Baber, Anne and Lynne Waymon, *Great Connections: Small Talk and Networking for Businesspeople*. Manassas Park, Va.: Impact Publications, 1992.

Blechman, Bruce and Jay Conrad Levinson, *Guerrilla Financing: Alternative Techniques to Financing Any Small Business*. Boston: Houghton Mifflin, 1991.

Booher, Dianna, *Clean Up Your Act! Effective Ways To Organize Paperwork—and Get It Out of Your Life*. New York: Warner Books, 1992.

Blades, William H., *Selling: The Mother of All Enterprise: Sure-Fire Tactics To Boost Sales and Survive Business Turmoil*. Phoenix, Ariz.: Marketing Methods Press, 1994.

Chapman, Elwood N., *Sales Training Basics: A Primer for Those New to Selling*. Menlo Park, Calif.: Crisp Publications, Inc., 1992.

Driscoll, Dawn-Marie and Carol R. Goldberg, *Members of the Club: The Coming of Age of Executive Women*. New York: The Free Press, 1993.

Edelston, Martin and Marion Buhagiar, *I Power: The Secrets of Great Business in Bad Times*. New York: Barricade Books, 1992.

Edwards, Paul and Sarah Edwards, *Working from Home: Everything You Need To Know About Living and Working Under the Same Roof*. New York: G.P. Putnam's Sons, 1994.

Fassel, Diane, *Working Ourselves to Death and the Rewards of Recovery*. New York: HarperPaperbacks, 1990.

Godfrey, Joline, *Our Wildest Dreams: Women Entrepreneurs Making Money, Having Fun, Doing Good*. New York: HarperBusiness, 1992.

Harragan, Betty Lehan, *Games Mother Never Taught You: Corporate Gamesmanship for Women*. New York: Warner Books, 1977.

King, Alfred M., *Total Cash Management: A Company-Wide System for Forecasting, Managing, and Improving Cash Flow*. New York: McGraw-Hill, Inc., 1994.

Larkin, Geraldine A., *Woman to Woman: Street Smarts for Women Entrepreneurs*. Englewood Cliffs, N.J.: Prentice Hall, 1993.

Lerner, Harriet G., *The Dance of Anger: A Woman's Guide to Changing the Patterns of Intimate Relationships*. New York: HarperPerennial, 1985.

Levine, Michael, *Guerrilla P.R.: How You Can Wage an Effective Publicity Campaign ... Without Going Broke*. New York: HarperBusiness, 1993.

Levinson, Jay Conrad, *Guerrilla Advertising: Cost-Effective Tactics for Small-Business Success*. Boston: Houghton Mifflin, 1994.

Maddox, Rebecca, *Inc. Your Dreams*. New York: Viking Press, 1995.

New York Publicity Outlets. New Milford, Conn.: Public Relations Plus, Inc., 1995.

Pinson, Linda and Jerry Jinnett, *Anatomy of a Business Plan*. Chicago: Enterprise Dearborn, 1993.

Pinson, Linda and Jerry Jinnett, *The Home-Based Entrepreneur*. Dover, N.H.: Upstart, 1993.

Pinson, Linda and Jerry Jinnett, *Keeping the Books*. Dover, N.H.: Upstart, 1993.

Radio Contacts. New York: BPI Media Services, 1995.

RoAne, Susan, *The Secrets of Savvy Networking: How To Make the Best Connections for Business and Personal Success*. New York: Warner Books, 1993.

Schiffman, Stephan, *The 25 Most Common Sales Mistakes ... and How To Avoid Them*. Holbrook, Mass.: Bob Adams, Inc., 1990.

The Standard Periodical Directory. New York: Oxbridge Communications, 1995.

Tannen, Deborah, *Talking from 9 to 5*. New York: William Morrow and Company, Inc., 1994.

Television Contacts. New York: BPI Media Services, 1995.
Smith, Jeanette, *The Publicity Kit*. New York: John Wiley & Sons, Inc., 1991.

Zuckerman, Laurie B., *On Your Own: A Woman's Guide to Building a Business*. Chicago: Upstart, 1990.

Health and Fitness

Suggested Reading

Diamond, Harvey and Marilyn Diamond, *Fit for Life*. New York: Warner Books, 1985.

Fenton, Mark and Seth Bauer, *The 90-Day Fitness Walking Program*. New York: Berkley, 1995.

Heller, Rachael F. and Richard F. Heller, *The Carbohydrate Addict's Diet: The Lifelong Solution to Yo Yo Dieting*. New York: Signet, 1991.

Martin, Barbara, *Relaxacise: The No Effort Exercise*. Birchgrove, Australia: Sally Milner Publishing, 1992.

Ornish, Dean, *Eat More, Weigh Less*. New York: HarperPerennial, 1993.

Pinckney, Callan, *Callanetics*. New York: Avon Books, 1984.

Ulene, Art, *Take It Off! Keep It Off!* Berkeley, Calif.: Ulysses Press, 1995.

Vedral, Joyce L., *Bottoms Up!* New York: Warner Books, 1993.

Vedral, Joyce L., *The Fat Burning Workout*. New York: Warner Books, 1991.

Vedral, Joyce L., *Now or Never*. New York: Warner Books, 1986.

Waterhouse, Debra, *Outsmarting the Female Fat Cell*. New York: Warner Books, 1993.

Webb, Tamilee, *Step Up Fitness Workout*. New York: Workman Publishing, 1994.

White, Timothy P., and the editors of the University of California at Berkeley Wellness Letter, *The Wellness Guide to Life-long Fitness*. New York: Rebus, 1993.

Suggested Videos

Before purchasing any of these videos, try renting first to see which ones are right for you.

Buns of Steel 2000, Maier Group.

Jane Fonda's Easy Going Workout, Lorimar Home Video.

Jane Fonda's Favorite Fat Burners, Vision Entertainment.

Karen Voight Firm Arms & Abs, Voight Video.

Kari Anderson Fitness Formula Step Aerobic and Abdominal Workout, A*Vision.

Kathy Smith: New Yoga, BodyVision.

Kathy Smith: Secrets of a Great Body: Upper Body Workout, BodyVision.

Kathy Smith: Secrets of a Great Body: Lower Body Workout, BodyVision.

Keli Roberts: Total Body Circuit Training Workout, CBS Fox Video.

Keli Roberts: The Ultimate Step Workout, CBS Fox Video.

Molly Fox: Total Body Workout, Sony Music Video.

Nike Total-Body Conditioning: Integrated Step and Sculpt, Nike, Inc.

Suggested Spas

When it's time to relax, a spa vacation will revitalize and energize you for your work as an entrepreneur.

The Peaks at Telluride, Telluride, Colo. (303-728-6800)

La Costa Resort and Spa, Carlsbad, Calif. (800-854-5000)

New Age Health Spa, Neversink, N.Y. (800-682-4348)

The Greenhouse, Arlington, Texas (817-640-4000)

Rancho La Puerta, Tecate, Mexico (800-443-7565)

Canyon Ranch, Tucson, Ariz. (800-726-9900)

Canyon Ranch in the Berkshires, Lenox, Mass. (800-726-9900)

Green Valley Spa and Tennis Resort, St. George, Utah (800-237-1068)

Golden Door, Escondido, Calif. (800-424-0777)

National Women's Associations and Organizations

Each of these organizations plays a distinctive role in helping women business owners by providing information, education, networking opportunities and more. Call the national headquarters of each group to obtain information about local chapters.

American Association of University Women, 1111 16th Street NW, Washington, DC 20036 (202-785-7700)

American Business Women's Association, 9100 Ward Parkway, P.O. Box 8728, Kansas City, MO 64114-0728 (816-361-6621)

National Association for Female Executives, 30 Irving Place, New York, NY 10003 (212-477-2200)

National Association of Women Business Owners, 1413 K Street NW, Suite 637, Washington, DC 20005 (301-608-2590)

National Chamber of Commerce for Women, 10 Waterside Place, Suite 6H, New York, NY 10010 (212-685-3454)

National Federation of Black Women Business Owners, 1500 Massachusetts Avenue NW, Suite 22, Washington, DC 20005 (202-833-3450)

National Federation of Business and Professional Women, 2012 Massachusetts Avenue NW, Washington, DC 20036 (202-293-1100)

Women in Management, 30 North Michigan Avenue, Suite 508, Chicago, IL 60602 (312-263-3636)

Training and Education

Women's Entrepreneurial Business Training

The following organizations provide business training courses for women entrepreneurs.

California American Woman's Economic Development Corporation, 230 Pine Avenue, Long Beach, CA 90802 (310-983-3747)

Women's Business Development Center, 8 South Michigan, Suite 400, Chicago, IL 60603 (312-853-3477)

Small Business Center, Fashion Institute of Technology, 27th Street at Seventh Avenue, New York, NY (212-760-7250)

National Education Center for Women in Business, Seton Hill College, Seton Hill Drive, Greensburg, PA 15602-1599 (412-830-4625 or 800-NECWB-4U)

American Woman's Economic Development Corporation, 71 Vanderbilt Avenue, Suite 320, New York, NY 10169 (212-692-9100 or 800-222-AWED)

Women's Initiative for Self-Employment, 450 Mission Street, Suite 402, San Francisco, CA 94105 (415-247-9473)

Women Entrepreneurs of Baltimore, Inc., 28 E. Ostend Street, Baltimore, MD 21230 (410-727-4921)

Graduate Schools

These graduate schools offer MBA programs with a concentration or courses in entrepreneurship.

Babson College, Graduate School of Business, Wellesley, Massachusetts (617-239-4320)

Harvard University, Graduate School of Business, Boston, Massachusetts (617-495-6127)

New York University, Stern School of Business, New York, New York (212-998-0100)

University of California at Los Angeles, The John E. Anderson Graduate School of Management, Los Angeles, California (310-825-6121)

University of Colorado at Boulder, Graduate School of Business, Boulder, Colorado (303-492-1831)

University of Pennsylvania, The Wharton School, Philadelphia, Pennsylvania (215-898-6183)

University of Southern California, School of Business Administration, Los Angeles, California (213-740-0641)

University of Texas at Austin, Graduate School of Business, Austin, Texas (512-471-7612)

Wichita State University, Wichita, Kansas (316-689-3000)

Index